All things being equal?

A practical guide to widening participation for adults with learning difficulties in continuing education

Jeannie Sutcliffe and Yola Jacobsen

NIACE
THE NATIONAL ORGANISATION

Published by the National Institute of
Adult Continuing Education (England and Wales)
21 De Montfort Street
Leicester LE1 7GE

Company registration no. 2603322
Charity registration no. 1002775

ISBN 1 86201 051 X

First published 1998

© 1998 National Institute of Adult Continuing Education (England and Wales)

NIACE
THE NATIONAL ORGANISATION
FOR ADULT LEARNING

NIACE, the national organisation for adult learning, has a
broad remit to promote lifelong learning opportunities for
adults. NIACE works to develop increased participation in
education and training, particularly for those who do not have
easy access because of barriers of class, gender, age, race,
language and culture, learning difficulties and disabilities, or
insufficient financial resources.

NIACE's website on the internet is http://www.niace.org.uk

SUPPORTED BY

JR
JOSEPH
ROWNTREE
FOUNDATION

The **Joseph Rowntree Foundation** has supported this
project as part of its programme of research and innovative
development projects, which it hopes will be of value to policy
makers and practitioners. The facts presented and views
expressed are, however, those of the author and not necessarily
those of the Foundation.

Cataloguing in Publications Data
A CIP record for this title is available from the British Library

Photographs: Kathie Bevan pvi and p22 ; Nick Hayes p49 and p73

Cover illustration: Chris Harman, © Artists at SITE, The City Lit, London
Cover printed in Great Britain by Russell Press, Nottingham

Designed and typeset by Boldface, London EC1
Printed and bound in Great Britain by Alden Press, Oxford

Contents

Acknowledgements

We would like to thank the people and places who have supported this project for their help. We are grateful to the Joseph Rowntree Foundation for supporting this project, and we appreciate the invaluable help of both Linda Ward, who advised us and commented helpfully on the final text, and Claire Benjamin, who gave us ongoing support and chaired the Research Advisory Group. Many thanks to:

Everyone who replied to our initial letter
People who attended and contributed to our network meetings
Alan Tuckett, NIACE, who was consistently supportive of the work
Anne Agius, NIACE, who gave us excellent secretarial support
Rob Hancock, who undertook our site visits in Wales
The Research Advisory Group members, who met regularly to give us helpful ideas:
Dorothy Atkinson, Open University
Janet Chadwick, Learning Support Manager, Manchester Adult Education Services
Ian Harris, Faculty Manager, Hertford Regional College
Neville Hayles, Consultant
John Lawton, National Education Officer, Mencap
Lynn Macqueen, (Observer) Education Programmes Officer, FEFC (East Midlands)
Jenny Orpwood, Development Worker, CHANGE
Frances Tucker, NATFHE
CHANGE consultants for their advice, support and contributions throughout the project:
Paul Adeline, Keith Dalgleish, Justine March, Richard West
All of the staff, students and organisations who hosted visits:
Anglia Polytechnic University; Blackburn College; Clarendon College, Nottingham; Coleg Menai, Bangor; College of North East London; Entelechy, London; Fosse Day Centre, Leicester/WEA East Midlands, Leicester; Hackney Community College; Hertford Regional College; Lambeth Accord; Lambeth Community Education; Leicester South Fields College; Manchester Adult Education Services; Northampton College; North Birmingham College; Oaklands College, Hertfordshire; Richmond Adult and Community College, London; Solihull College; South Nottingham College; Southwark Adult Education.

Foreword

As the Minister with responsibility for disabled people, I very much look forward to implementing the Government's commitment to comprehensive and enforceable civil rights in this area. The Disability Rights Task Force is vital to this commitment, since its work ranges across all aspects of life and society.

I am sure that a key way in which disabled people will reach their full potential is through having the best possible access to education and training. Although many schools, colleges and universities have made great strides in recent years in improving provision for disabled students, I believe there is still some way to go. We have not yet developed a fully inclusive approach to learning, in which the individual needs of the learner are paramount.

I therefore welcome this publication, and am delighted to offer this foreword. The book will be of value to all those who work with adults with learning difficulties in further education. I hope that readers will note the good practice it contains, and consider how they may put this into practical effect.

MARGARET HODGE
Parliamentary Under-Secretary of State for
Employment and Equal Opportunities

August 1998

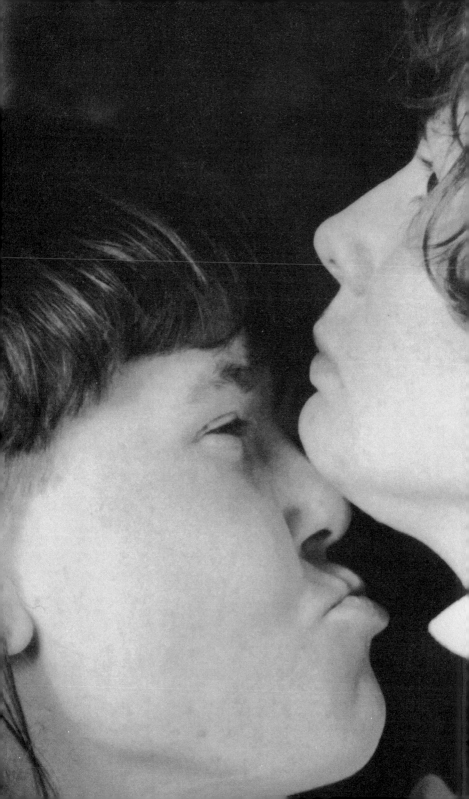

I

Introduction

This book celebrates good practice in continuing education for marginalised groups of adults with learning difficulties. At the same time, the book highlights major gaps in provision for these learners. Much of the good practice identified during the project was fragile and we hope that by describing the work, it may help both to safeguard existing provision and to provide a resource for planning new developments.

What is the book about?

Equal opportunities is a term which is widely used. What does it mean for adults with learning difficulties who want to access learning? Equal rights to take part in learning should be available for *all* adults with learning difficulties, regardless of race, gender, disability or age. This book sets out to describe examples of education for individuals and groups of people with learning difficulties who can often be marginalised from the education system. It describes examples of provision for people with learning difficulties who, for example:
- are older
- have profound/multiple learning difficulties
- are from black or other minority ethnic groups
- are women
- present what is described as 'challenging' behaviour

- have sensory disabilities
- have a dual label of learning difficulties and mental health difficulties
- have a history of institutionalisation.

Who is this book for?

This book is designed to support people who want to develop learning opportunities for adults with learning difficulties who have often missed out on appropriate education, for example those with profound and multiple learning difficulties or those from black and other minority ethnic groups. This book is aimed at managers, tutors and lecturers working with adults who have learning difficulties in colleges of further education and in adult education services. It will also be of interest to staff working with adults who have learning difficulties in other settings such as social services, health and voluntary organisations. The book may also be of interest to parents, relatives and carers of adults with learning difficulties.

How can this book be used?

We hope that this book will be a useful resource for people who want to develop continuing education provision for under-represented groups of adults with learning difficulties. Examples from existing practice are used to describe issues and themes that arise, along with quotes from students where possible. There are checklists, summaries and resource suggestions at the end of each chapter. The concluding chapter offers suggestions for action.

In designing the format of this book, we decided that to have a separate chapter on each group of learners would be counter-productive, and would only serve to reinforce the isolation which some of these learners experience. Many of the issues are shared: for example, getting access, staff support and accessible information. We have, therefore, drawn out key themes as chapter headings, and readers will find examples of different case studies interspersed throughout the text.

About this opening chapter

This chapter looks at:
* why the project *All Things Being Equal?* was undertaken and what it aimed to do
* key features of interesting practice for the project visits
* recent policy initiatives of relevance.

Background to the work

Why was this research done?

In 1996, the National Institute of Adult Continuing Education (NIACE) published *Still A Chance to Learn?* (Sutcliffe and Macadam), which addressed the impact of the Further and Higher Education Act (1992) on continuing education for adults with learning difficulties. This research was carried out by NIACE in collaboration with the Norah Fry Research Centre at the University of Bristol and was supported by the Joseph Rowntree Foundation. The research showed that provision for certain groups, such as older adults and those with profound and multiple learning difficulties, had diminished since the advent of the legislation. People told us that they feared that the new emphasis on accreditation and progression could exclude some groups of learners. The curriculum range had also narrowed, with a clear focus on what could be funded by the Further Education Funding Council (FEFC). Some courses such as music, art and drama had been axed in favour of vocational and basic skills courses.

NIACE has always had a commitment to under-represented groups of learners. We could see that the most vulnerable groups of learners had been subject to cuts. We drew up the proposal for the project *All Things Being Equal?*, which was welcomed and supported by the Joseph Rowntree Foundation. The findings of the project form the basis for this book.

The equal rights agenda

The campaign for equal rights for people with learning difficulties can be allied to the equal rights agenda for other groups. Civil rights are a key issue for black people, women and disabled people, as well as for lesbians and gays. The civil rights agenda extends to education too. It was only in 1971 that children with learning difficulties were legally allowed access to schools after being formerly described as 'ineducable'. In 1996, Robert Parkinson was refused funding by the Further Education Funding Council to go to a specialist residential college. Robert was aged 19 at the time of the appeal. The FEFC legal case was that Robert's profound/multiple learning difficulties made it unlikely that he would demonstrate progression in his learning, as required by the Further and Higher Education Act (1992) legislation. The LEA and Social Services did not fund his college place either, and Robert was unable to take up his place at college.

Racism, sexism and negative attitudes towards disability still affect people's chances of participating in learning. For people with learning difficulties who are, for example, black, Asian, deaf or wheelchair users, getting an appropriate education is that much harder.

The values which underpin the work are that all adults with learning difficulties have the right to join in with continuing education and to be a part of the learning community. Citizenship and inclusion in society are important human rights. Adults with learning difficulties have often been marginalised as a group of people. This marginalisation is compounded for some individuals with learning difficulties by racism, ageism and prejudice based on gender and disability.

What did the research aim to do?

The research set out to document innovative ways of working with particular groups or individuals with learning difficulties who are often marginalised or excluded from continuing education. Information about the project was sent to all FE Colleges and LEAs in England and Wales, inviting people to reply with details of any relevant provision they had for marginalised groups of students with learning difficulties. There were just over 160 replies and from these, 18 places were chosen for case study visits to gather material about the positive benefits and the challenges of developing such provision. Learners were asked what their views and perceptions were as an important part of this process.

Key features of interesting practice for the project

We chose a range of provision to visit in colleges, LEAs and voluntary organisations which offered some or all of the following key features of good practice:

- valuing diversity: respecting difference and welcoming learners accordingly
- established provision for specific groups or individuals from marginalised groups of adults with learning difficulties
- working in partnership with other organisations
- individually tailored learning
- imaginative examples of curriculum development
- provision in a range of settings, to include outreach work in day centres, hospitals and secure units.

T

We would also endorse the key features of successful provision outlined in the FEFC's Good Practice Report (December 1996) on *Provision for Students with Learning Difficulties and/or Disabilities*, which includes in addition to our list above the need for appropriate assessment, specialist support, checks on learning and quality, the involvement of senior managers and staff training.

Staff network meetings

Our perception from *Still A Chance to Learn?* was that managers and practitioners working with marginalised groups could feel quite isolated so, as part of the *All Things Being Equal?* project, three network meetings were held to enable colleagues to meet and share information and ideas.

Seizing the opportunity – what recent policy initiatives have relevance?

The broad focus of *All Things Being Equal?* was to highlight developments for under-represented groups of learners who have learning difficulties. A number of relevant reports have recently been published and can be used to support the case for developing provision for marginalised groups of adults with learning difficulties. They make useful background reading and can provide helpful references if the case to develop provision needs arguing.

Inclusive Learning (1996, FEFC)

This major report outlines many substantive recommendations to improve education for adults with learning difficulties and/or disabilities. The report was the outcome of a three-year committee of enquiry chaired by Professor John Tomlinson and commissioned by the Further Education Funding Council. A consultation exercise by FEFC in 1997 showed widespread support for the major recommendations in the report. Among the recommendations are that provision should be established for three groups of learners who are currently under-represented:

- people with profound and multiple learning difficulties
- people with emotional/behavioural difficulties
- people with mental health difficulties.

The Further Education Funding Council is currently planning how to take these recommendations forward. In relation to *All Things Being Equal?*, profound and multiple learning difficulties are of relevance, while the other two groups highlighted by *Inclusive Learning* are relevant for those individuals who also have learning difficulties. The FEFC has set up an Inclusive Learning Steering Group, which is meeting six times a year to oversee developments in the implementation of the recommendations from the *Inclusive Learning* report. It was recognised that staff development is vitally needed to underpin developments: in 1997/8, FEFC committed £1 million to develop the 'Quality Initiative'. Nine colleges in England each acted as lead colleges to eight or nine other organisations. A second phase is in the planning stage at the time of writing. One of the proposed outcomes is a comprehensive set of materials for national staff development and possible accreditation.

The title and ethos of the *Inclusive Learning* report has caused some confusion amongst practitioners, as it does not in fact mean integrated learning but instead the concept of matching the student to the learning, which may or may not mean an integrated setting. As Professor Tomlinson writes in the introduction of *Inclusive Learning*:

> Our concept of inclusive learning is not synonymous with integration ... The first step is to determine the best possible learning environment, given the individual student and learning task.
> (1996, HMSO, p.5)

Mapping Provision (1997, FEFC)

In recognising that comprehensive data was missing, the Tomlinson Committee commissioned a detailed mapping exercise of further education for people with learning difficulties and/or disabilities. The findings showed that:

- female students with learning difficulties were slightly under-represented in the student population
- 50.8% of students were over 25. (However, there were no details given of older learners. The age breakdown of students was not shown in detail.)
- 'white students with learning difficulties were somewhat over-represented and non-white students correspondingly under-represented'
- people with profound and/or complex disabilities had been turned away by some colleges
- physical resource constraints, staffing, lack of equipment or personal constraints were cited as reasons for refusing disabled students.

The press release accompanying the launch of the report claimed that colleges could be catering for twice as many disabled students

Learning Works (1997, FEFC)

Helena Kennedy QC chaired a committee for the Further Education Funding Council on the topic of widening participation in further education. The report argues that we need to invest in adults who have been missing out on educational opportunities. The report is not specific to learning difficulties, but ensuing developments to widen participation may well have a spin-off for marginalised groups of adults with learning difficulties.

Learning for the Twenty-First Century (1997)

This report was produced by the National Advisory Group for Continuing Education and Lifelong Learning, chaired by Professor Bob Fryer. It makes the case for extending learning to include under-represented groups, and makes specific reference to developing opportunities for people with learning difficulties. Bob Fryer is passionate in arguing the case for expanding opportunities. At a NIACE conference (3 December 1997), he said:

'We need to think about the learning 'have nots'... we have been working with a system based on hierarchy, exclusion and failure and we must change this.'

These sentiments certainly ring true in relation to the experience of many excluded groups of people with learning difficulties.

The Learning Age (1998)

A green paper on lifelong learning for adults was issued in February 1998, with a consultation period to the end of July 1998. *The Learning Age* makes a few explicit references to people with learning difficulties and/or disabilities, notably in section 4.36. The proposed recommendations in this paragraph relate to improving access to continuing education in collaboration with voluntary and statutory bodies, to include people with severe learning difficulties, and building on the *Inclusive Learning* report.

Disability Discrimination Act and Disability Rights Task Force

Under the Disability Discrimination Act, colleges and LEAs are now required to present information about provision for disabled students. Meanwhile, the Disability Rights Task Force is advising the current government on civil rights for disabled people. Legislation is planned for a disability rights commission.

What did we find?

The next chapter gives an overview of our main findings, and is followed by a number of chapters on specific themes. The final chapter summarises main ideas for action.

▶ Summary

Earlier research called 'Still A Chance to Learn?' showed that certain groups of learners were missing out, such as those with profound and multiple learning difficulties.

This was backed up by data from the FEFC publications *Inclusive Learning* and *Mapping Provision*.

Site visits were made to a range of colleges, LEAs and voluntary organisations for the project. We looked for key features such as celebrating diversity and a multi-agency approach.

Recent policy initiatives and publications such as *Learning Works*, *Learning for the Twenty-First Century* and *The Learning Age* advocate the concept of widening participation in adult learning. These initiatives are for all learners, but may have important spin-offs for adults with learning difficulties.

Making it happen – a checklist of ideas

▶ Have you considered what impact the Further and Higher Education Act (1992) had on your area of work?

▶ Have you been able to read and brief colleagues about the Tomlinson report *Inclusive Learning*?

▶ Are you aware of key messages from relevant policy papers on adult learning, such as *Widening Participation* and *The Learning Age*?

REFERENCES/RESOURCES

The Learning Age: a renaissance for a new Britain, DfEE (1998, The Stationery Office)

Adults and the learning age, Briefing paper on *The Learning Age* (1998, NIACE)

Inclusive Learning: Report of the Learning Difficulties & Disabilities Committee(1996, HMSO Books)

How important is inclusive learning?, Briefing paper (1996, NIACE)

Macadam, M. and Sutcliffe, J. *Still A Chance To Learn?* A report of a project on the impact of the Further & Higher Education Act (1992) on education for adults with learning difficulties (1996, NIACE)

Mapping Provision, Report prepared by the Institute for Employment Studies (1997, The Stationery Office)

Helena Kennedy QC *Learning Works: Widening Participation in Further Education* (1997, FEFC)

Professor R. H. Fryer *Learning for the Twenty First Century* First report of the National Advisory Group for Continuing Education and Lifelong Learning (1997, DfEE)

Provision for Students with Learning Difficulties and /or Disabilities Good practice report (1996, FEFC)

FURTHER READING

NIACE has published a number of books and packs on education for adults with learning difficulties. Further guidance on good practice can be found in these publications:

Sutcliffe J. *Adults with Learning Difficulties: Education for Choice and Empowerment* (1990, NIACE and Open University Press)

Sutcliffe J. *Integration for Adults with Learning Difficulties* (1992, NIACE)

Sutcliffe J. and Simons K. *Self-Advocacy and Adults with Learning Difficulties* (1993, NIACE)

Sutcliffe J. *Teaching Basic Skills to Adults with Learning Difficulties* (1994, NIACE and the Basic Skills Agency)

Sutcliffe J. *Towards Inclusion: Developing Integrated Education for Adults with Learning Difficulties* (1996, NIACE)

Sutcliffe J. *Enabling Learning: A Student-centred Approach to Teaching Adults with Learning Difficulties* (1996, NIACE)

Sutcliffe J. and CHANGE *Training for Change: A Pack to Support Adults with Learning Difficulties to Develop the Skills to Become Trainers* (1998)

NIACE has also published titles on a range of topics, including mental health, adults who are deaf or hard of hearing, black learners and older learners. A full publications list is available from:

NIACE
21 De Montfort Street
Leicester LE1 7GE
Tel: 0116 204 4200/1

2

Overview of main findings

The main findings are summarised in this chapter, which is then followed by chapters which explore key themes and issues in more depth. Classes were visited in colleges, local education authorities and voluntary organisations. Discussions were held with students with learning difficulties, tutors, managers, parents and staff from other agencies. What did we find out during the course of the project?

Provision exists but is rare and often fragile

We were able to find isolated examples of provision for adults with learning difficulties who:

- were older
- had profound/multiple learning difficulties
- were from black or other minority ethnic groups
- were women
- presented what was described as 'challenging' behaviour
- had sensory disabilities
- had a dual label of learning difficulties and mental health difficulties
- had a history of institutionalisation.

However, these examples were relatively rare. Indeed, some of the examples we found were so fragile that their existence from term to term was in doubt. Provision was also dispersed and we had to make a large number of visits to different places to find examples of provision for all of the above individuals or groups of learners. Places which had developed provision tended to have specialised in one or two areas of work rather than offering opportunities for all of the learners listed above. However, one or two colleges with a fully inclusive approach were dealing with individuals who had a wide range of learning difficulties and disabilities.

Learners valued their courses

Students with learning difficulties from marginalised groups told us why they liked learning:

'I can say what I think.'

'I think it is good for me, I have had a good year.'

'The tutor can listen and help.'

'You can learn about different people. It's all right.'

'We looked at maps of different countries like Jamaica. I've been to Jamaica with my Mum for my birthday treat. I've got a cousin there.'

'I make friends here and meet people…The teachers are good, they are nice and they talk to me. I have to speak to the teacher about my courses and enrol here.'

'I like doing courses that help me to learn about the things I like to do.'

Access and support were often barriers

The biggest barrier to access was the lack of provision nationally, coupled with a lack of awareness in relation to the marginalised groups and individuals which the project looked at. Few access routes into education were available. The absence of appropriate opportunities gave a clear and negative message. One tutor summed it up by saying: 'People feel provision is not for them'.

General access issues included a lack of physical access for students with mobility difficulties, transport problems and inaccessible information. Although much of the support that did exist was excellent, there were several examples of support workers from other agencies being changed every week and thus disrupting continuity.

There were some positive examples of the curriculum being tailored to suit learners

We found examples where staff were working creatively to develop an appropriate curriculum, as the following examples show:

An Asian Studies course was set up at one college for adults with learning difficulties. The college has an Asian principal.

An arts course for black adults with learning difficulties was established. Cultural identity and self-image were an important part of the course.

One college has well-developed provision for adults with profound and multiple learning difficulties. Art, making musical instruments and coppicing are a few of the learning activities, which are all taught by subject specialists.

Ownership and a sense of belonging was crucial for students from marginalised groups

Helping black students to 'feel culture' through art and drama was an important aspect of the black arts group which was visited. Meanwhile, one group for deaf adults with learning difficulties has taken off since appointing a deaf tutor. The group meets at a centre used by deaf people, and members are realising that they belong to and are a part of the deaf community. This has widened their experience.

Practitioners and managers working with marginalised groups of students with learning difficulties often felt isolated

As one tutor put it: 'This is the very start of things that should be happening in this area... we're all working slightly isolated.' Her feelings were reflected by a number of other people we talked to.

When we held three network meetings for the project in late 1997, it was to give colleagues a chance to stand back from their work and to exchange information and ideas for mutual support. One person wrote on their evaluation form: 'Above all I feel that giving people a space and some quality time to discuss issues affecting them with others encountering the same difficulties was the most valuable experience – the realisation that you are not alone and the opportunity to restore your sanity!'

Some staff faced opposition from colleagues. In a few cases, people doing innovative work were always having to justify their work to sceptical colleagues, who seemed unconvinced that these areas of work merited dedicated resources and staffing. One person working with black adults with learning difficulties said: 'We have to fight for the fact that it is important and necessary.'

Some potential learners faced multiple discrimination

The odds of finding appropriate provision were harder if people had more than one 'label' to contend with. For example, we did not find much provision for Asian women with learning difficulties. One of the best examples we found was actually in the context of a small voluntary organisation. The book *Double Discrimination* (1990, Baxter, Poonia, Ward and Nadirshaw) describes issues for services in general in relation to people with learning difficulties from black and minority ethnic communities. The sole example in that book of a college course for black women with learning difficulties, tutored by black staff, closed down soon after the book was published. Some people may even face threefold discrimination in seeking appropriate provision, such as the man with learning difficulties who is also deaf and black. People with the dual diagnosis of both learning difficulties and mental health difficulties also tend to miss out. Rather than just double discrimination, some people face multiple oppression.

Funding varies and accreditation can pose challenges

Funding came from a number of sources, including the FEFCs and LEAs, as well as support from Social Services departments, Health Trusts and voluntary organisations. Some funding was short-term and vulnerable to cuts. One local authority made large cuts to its well-established outreach work at about the time of our visits, which affected community-based provision for learners from marginalised groups.

Funding and accreditation were seen as closely linked for Further Education Funding Council (FEFC)-funded provision, as is prescribed in the relevant legislation. The emphasis on accreditation was not always seen as appropriate for marginalised groups of learners. As one person said forcefully: 'It's accreditate, not educate!'

In one case, a course had been developed which was not accredited, although it did monitor progression. Although such a course would in theory be eligible for FEFC funding, we were told that 'the computer software threw it out'. We heard a similar story from another source. These were rare instances, but demonstrate that even occasional hiccups at a local level can cause great difficulty in developing provision for marginalised students. It also raises issues of staff feeling even more isolated and the need for training in successfully putting data onto the relevant forms.

Working across agencies was essential

Working across agencies has always been important in education for adults with learning difficulties. We found that for marginalised groups, it was an essential part of developing new provision. Partners from different organisations identified needs in common and then devised a joint strategy for action:

> One college set up provision for adults with profound/multiple learning difficulties in close collaboration with Social Services. Social Services staff go into college as support workers and college staff also deliver education at day centres.
>
> A development worker setting up a group for black adults with learning difficulties had to liaise with a range of community groups to find potential learners, who often did not use traditional services. Social Services recently set up a local drop-in facility aimed at this group, and work closely with the adult education worker.
>
> One private organisation offers provision for people with the dual diagnosis of learning difficulties and mental health difficulties on site at a college. Partnership with the college and other agencies was imperative.

Language and labels could be confusing

It is difficult to describe or define precisely what we mean by certain terms. For example, the term 'challenging behaviour' may be understood very differently by colleges and by Social Services, who may tolerate different levels of behaviour. One tutor with considerable experience compared perceptions of teachers of people with learning difficulties with teachers at a comprehensive school in relation to the term 'challenging behaviour'. The former recounted examples of biting, kicking, scratching and masturbating in public...the latter described cheekiness, smoking and talking in class. This shows the impact of different contexts and interpretations of the same term.

The confusion about what it means to have both learning difficulties and mental health difficulties, or a lack of understanding of profound and multiple learning difficulties, may be a factor in these groups being overlooked. Similarly, when we asked about provision for older adults, some people had different perceptions about what 'older' meant. One person asked: 'Do you mean people over 27?'

There was a small but real risk of violence by students

There were several instances of violence reported to us, where staff had been threatened or hit by students who were upset. One place which taught people who had both learning difficulties and mental health difficulties issued walkie-talkies to staff for emergencies and also trained them in restraint techniques. In contrast, in one class visited, the support worker spent some time filing her nails and then fell asleep. A violent outburst by a student later followed, in which the tutor was assaulted. Could better quality support have deflected this incident? Strategies for dealing with the possibility of violence by a very small minority of students include staff training to develop relevant skills, combined with effective student support.

Staff development and training in relation to marginalised groups was under-developed

We asked people what staff development and training was offered. Most places had something going, but the overall picture is that it is an under-developed hotch-potch. People were doing bits and pieces here and there, but the lack of a coherent and structured national strategy was evident. The current Further Education Funding Council (FEFC) 'Quality Initiative' is designed to remedy this and to provide an over-arching national training and accreditation system for colleges of further education in England. We welcome the fact that Phase 2 of this initiative will be accessible to staff working in LEAs. We hope that it will address working with under-represented groups. Developments in Wales will also be an issue as these are not covered by the initiative.

▶ **Summary**

Examples of provision do exist for adults with learning difficulties from marginalised groups, but they are rare and often fragile.

Limited access to learning opportunities and the lack of appropriate support were often barriers to participation.

Practitioners and managers often felt isolated, while innovative provision was sometimes under-valued and needed to be continually justified.

Some potential learners faced multiple discrimination. For example a person who is deaf, black and has learning difficulties may face a number of barriers.

Funding varies: sources of funding included FEFC and LEAs, as well as Social Services departments, Health Trusts and voluntary organisations. Some funding was short-term and vulnerable to cuts. Accreditation was not always accessible or relevant for all learners.

Working across agencies is essential and was a pre-requisite for much of the provision visited.

Language and labels can be confusing and this factor may have some bearing on provision being under-developed.

There were some positive examples of the curriculum being tailored to suit learners.

Staff development and training in relation to marginalised groups is under-developed. The FEFC 'Quality Initiative' plans to set up a national training and accreditation framework for inclusive learning in colleges of further education which may help.

Making it happen – a checklist of ideas

▶ What provision is currently offered to learners from marginalised groups in your area?

▶ What are the barriers and how could they be overcome?

▶ What equal opportunities strategies exist that developments could be linked into?

REFERENCES/RESOURCES

C. Baxter, K. Poonia, L. Ward and Z. Nadirshaw, *Double Discrimination* (1990, King's Fund Centre/Commission for Racial Equality).

3

Getting access

'We all need access to things. People with learning difficulties need access in all sorts of different ways. It is important that people with learning difficulties have greater access in places where they work and visit.'

This comment from Richard West, a black, deaf man with a learning difficulty who works as a consultant, highlights that there are a variety of ways in which people with learning difficulties need access. Although access usually brings to mind transport and ways to physically get into buildings, there are many other aspects of access relevant for adults with learning difficulties who want to use services. This chapter will address a range of issues to do with adults with learning difficulties from marginalised groups gaining access to education.

Access at all?

Attitudes

Many adults with learning difficulties have to rely on their support staff (or key workers) to initiate and organise activities.

This dependency inevitably means that they will be influenced and guided by their supporters' values and attitudes. Staff may make assumptions about older people or be unaware of the importance of the cultural needs of people from minority ethnic backgrounds. This dependency on staff is increased for a person who has profound and multiple learning difficulties. As one person with a learning difficulty commented about residential staff: 'They may not tell potential students about what is on offer...'

- One study, *Fair Shares for All?* (1996, Walker, Ryan and Walker), has shown that staff felt that skills training was less relevant for older people with learning difficulties than for younger people with learning difficulties. Staff were less confident about older people's capacity to learn than younger people.

Attitudes of staff in continuing education

The attitudes of education staff can also be a barrier:

- A lecturer working with students with learning difficulties and mental health problems pointed out that mental health was not yet included in the college's Disability Statement. She felt that this was indicative of a lack of awareness of mental health issues where she worked. The college needed to take a whole-college approach over such issues, develop policy and train staff to raise awareness.
- A member of staff in one adult education service, who set up a group for black students with learning difficulties as an access route into adult education, frequently had to justify the existence of the group to her colleagues:

'People usually say, "Oh it's just for black students is it?", so you have to be prepared to explain why so that the person goes away with a positive answer.'

Opportunities to learn

People may have been in situations throughout their lives where access to education has not been possible. It was only in 1971 that legislation stopped referring to children with learning difficulties as 'ineducable'. Many older people, when younger, will have been labelled in this way. People with learning difficulties who have spent a large part of their lives living in long-stay hospitals will have been deprived of opportunities, including a chance to be a student in continuing education.

Some deaf students with learning difficulties have left school with no or poor signing and reading skills. Education has denied them access to any coherent form of communication. This is now being addressed in one area of the north west through adult education classes for deaf students with learning difficulties, who are taught signing by deaf tutors.

There are a few examples of students with profound and multiple learning difficulties having access to continuing education. However, some people clearly feel that this is not appropriate:

Professor Tomlinson, chair of the FEFC Learning Difficulties and/or Disabilities Committee, told a national conference of one person's reaction to including people with profound and multiple learning difficulties in continuing education. It was of disbelief that education authorities wanted to bother with that kind of person.

Physical access

Older people with learning difficulties, and people with profound and multiple learning difficulties in particular, rely on wheelchair and easy physical access to college and adult education facilities. Whilst the FEFC has an ongoing programme of supporting colleges to make buildings accessible, many older buildings used by adult and community education still struggle to provide access with very limited funds.

Staff try and 'make do' in difficult circumstances and often (rather than not have a class at all) classes are moved to areas where students who are already marginalised become even more isolated.

One community education centre which was visited as part of the fieldwork for this project held a class for students with profound and multiple learning difficulties in an accessible portable cabin in the grounds of the main building. The students in the group who used wheelchairs could not use the other facilities of the centre such as the canteen, which was on the first floor of the main building. To keep the group together, the tutor made arrangements for the students to make tea in the classroom. This class became an isolated group within the centre, losing the chance to mix with and meet other students. However, the only other option would have been to not run the class at this centre at all.

Poor physical access can stop people attending classes:

- A student with profound and multiple learning difficulties who uses a wheelchair could only attend her yoga class if there were two support workers to lift her wheelchair down a few steps into the hall where her class was held. Once she was in the class, the student needed the support of only one of the workers. Due to staffing levels at her house, often there were not two staff available to take her to class and consequently this student attended classes infrequently. All involved found this very frustrating. If there had been a small ramp for the steps, the problem could have been resolved. People with profound and multiple learning difficulties may also need access to changing facilities. Finding appropriate space for this can be a difficulty.
- One college has a Student's Disability Action Group which reports directly to the Principal about issues, including physical access, which concern them.

Information

CHANGE consultant Paul Adeline makes t

'It is important to have access to information, because having accessible information gives people with learning difficulties more power.'

Language and format

Information about courses is most commonly available in written form in a prospectus, making it inaccessible to anybody who doesn't read. Information is usually written with parents/carers in mind and there is not always an accessible version available.

Some colleges and LEAs do make information more accessible to students by using symbols, illustrations and photos. Staff make time to sit with students when they come in to enrol for a class and go through the information with them.

A specially made video prospectus could be helpful for people with learning difficulties generally and accessible for deaf students with learning difficulties. Blind and partially-sighted students can use a prospectus on tape. Audio and video tapes in different languages have also been found to be the best way of providing information for people from minority ethnic communities, when backed up with outreach work from staff who can tell people about the service.

- A black worker with learning difficulties from CHANGE suggested that colleges could produce clear accessible information, maybe a video of black students at college:

'...to prove that people can do it. They can see the video and think, "I want to do the same".'

.ACE and CHANGE are producing a *Training for Change* pack for people with learning difficulties who want to train to be trainers. So as not to exclude people who don't read, deaf people with learning difficulties and blind people with learning difficulties, the pack is being produced with illustrations, a video, and audio-tapes to accompany it.

• CHANGE is making information more accessible for their workers by illustrating all their written text. Pictures are being collected in a picture bank and scanned into a computer. CHANGE also has a word bank which gives clear definitions of frequently used words or phrases.

• Gwynedd Council produces a leaflet in Welsh and English, with details of reading books which are a resource of the basic skills service for adults with learning difficulties. The leaflet is in large print with illustrations.

Terminology

Using jargon can make information difficult to understand. This can be particularly hard if you do not speak or read English. Translating information has to be done appropriately. As one Asian lecturer pointed out:

'When you are translating publicity you have to translate it to the right pitch, not too formal.'

Distribution

People with learning difficulties often have to rely on families or carers to tell them what is happening at the local college or adult education centre, as information is often not given directly to the student. As one student commented:

'...a lot of people don't have access to information...probably staff get it.'

In a study of Asian people with learning difficulties, parents said it was important to leave information in public places such as doctor's surgeries. Other places to leave information to reach as many people as possible could be community centres and day services. (Hatton, 1996)

Transport

We all know how frustrating it is when the car doesn't start, the bus is late or the train breaks down, and the control we had over our journey suddenly disappears. Most of us can make other arrangements or, if we have to, resign ourselves to the fact that we are going to be late. However, transport to and from classes is the key to access for many students with learning difficulties who always have to rely on others to support them when they are travelling. Older people with learning difficulties and people with profound and multiple learning difficulties in particular will often not be independent travellers.

People who live in rural areas can be very restricted by the lack of transport:

A deaf student with learning difficulties living in an isolated rural area was only able to get to college on one day of the week. Staff arranged her timetable for the day so she could do as many classes as possible in that day.

Transport needs to be flexible

Students with learning difficulties often rely on transport from their day centre to get to college. Day centres have to organise complicated transport timetables to accommodate as many of their clients as possible. Unfortunately, this can mean that the transport is run to fit the schedule of the day service as a whole and not of the student.

- On one of the project visits for this study a student, travelling in a minibus from his day centre, arrived a half hour late and had to leave ten minutes early, missing a total of forty minutes of his two-hour class.
- Students from one day centre couldn't get to their classes at all for several weeks because the minibus they were using on a temporary basis was too wide to get down the drive to the college.

There are some schemes being developed to support people with learning difficulties to travel which encourage as much independence as possible and the use of public/community-based transport rather than 'special' transport:

- Hackney Community Transport is linking with Social Services to develop a service for people with disabilities travelling to college as part of their Plus Bus Scheme. Travel training is part of this scheme, as is a training programme for the drivers. A person with learning difficulties will be trained to be one of the trainers on this programme. Bus passes have been designed with a picture of the college and the student. Maps with illustrations, clock faces and a clear picture of the route are also being designed.

- CHANGE has a campaign to make information about transport in London more accessible. Amongst other things, the campaign is hoping to develop tube maps and bus timetables which are more accessible.

- Haringey Disabilities Consortium has a transport advocate whose job is to research the transport needs of people with learning difficulties and support people to use public/community transport.

Fees

People with learning difficulties are often on low incomes and are among the poorest groups in society. The cost of studying in some cases can be a barrier. Often there are concessions available on fees but there may also be costly class materials to pay for. This could be the case for classes such as photography and flower arranging.

▶ Summary

Basic rights such as access to information, choice and education have frequently been denied to people with learning difficulties. Some groups have missed out more than others.

In continuing education, it is important that the particular needs of marginalised groups of people with learning difficulties are recognised, whether due to culture, age, gender or the nature of the disability.

One of the key ways in which these groups are excluded is in relation to getting access to learning in the first place. This includes initially finding out about classes, getting transport and physical access into the venue.

Making it happen – a checklist of ideas

Disability Statements

▶ Are there any gaps in the Disability Statement where you work regarding marginalised groups of students with learning difficulties?

▶ Could you use this as an opportunity to open a discussion and raise awareness with management and other colleagues?

▶ How could you involve students in this discussion and could you develop training sessions and include students as trainers?

▶ Is the Statement presented in different accessible formats?

Physical access

▶ Does poor physical access exclude any students from classes?

▶ Are there any pieces of equipment, such as a mobile ramp, that would help?

▶ If so, can you apply for funding from the Equal Opportunities Committees, Property Committee or from other places for such equipment?

▶ How could students themselves speak to college management about such barriers to access?

Information

▶ How accessible is the information for students with learning difficulties from marginalised groups?

▶ Could students do their own survey and suggest changes and improvements and be involved in producing information?

▶ Have you any contacts in the local community who could advise you on accessible information and its distribution?

Transport

▶ Are there any local community transport teams you could work with to develop transport schemes?

▶ Could you work with students to make maps and timetables accessible?

REFERENCES/RESOURCES

Walker, Ryan and Walker *Fair Shares for All?* (1996, Pavilion Publishing in association with the Joseph Rowntree Foundation)

Hatton, C. *Services for Asian Adults with learning disabilities and their families: the views of users and carers* (1996, Hester Adrian Centre, Manchester)

The RNIB See it Right leaflets give guidance on making information accessible by using clear print, video, audio tape and advise how to develop a policy for access to information for blind and partially sighted people. Contact Gill Levy at RNIB, 224 Great Portland Street, London WIN 6AA.

CHANGE are putting their picture bank on to CD Rom which will be on sale in 1998. Contact CHANGE, First Floor, 69-85 Old Street, London EC1V 9HY.

4

Tailoring the curriculum: race, ethnicity, gender and age

Issues for people with learning difficulties from black and other minority ethnic groups

'There should be more groups for black people with learning difficulties.'

'I have the right to learn about my history and culture.'

(1993, Black People First)

Five years on from the words spoken above and there has been little progress in reaching potential learners from black and other minority ethnic groups. We found very few examples of provision aimed at people with learning difficulties from black or Asian communities. This reinforces the data from *Mapping Provision* (FEFC, 1997) that students with learning difficulties from black and other minority ethnic groups are under-represented. 'What black students with learning difficulties?' as one learning support manager at a large city college, herself black, said ironically.

Why is such provision important? It can provide a chance to:

- share culture and identity
- celebrate positive images and role models
- learn about self-advocacy in a supportive environment
- learn from shared experiences of being, for example, Asian women with learning difficulties
- follow an access route into continuing education
- progress to other learning opportunities.

Recent research looked at services for South Asian adults with learning difficulties and found that 'we know surprisingly little about services for Asian adults with learning difficulties and their families. Yet supporting this group of people should be a high priority... the demand for adult services will rise dramatically, with current projections estimating that the number of Asian adults with learning difficulties will more than double over the next decade.' (1997, Hatton *et al*) Surely we should be setting up appropriate provision now, especially in anticipation of this rise in numbers?

The Black Vision Workshop, Manchester

'I do art, painting, and drawing and singing.'
(Student at the Black Vision Workshop)

This pilot course was set up by Gillian Kelly, a black arts development worker, and is funded by the Local Education Authority. The course was set up in response to the lack of participation by black adults with learning difficulties in the adult education service. The course offers black adults with learning difficulties the chance to do a range of creative arts, which have included:

- going to hear a band from Zaire
- sketching in the local park
- mixing paints to make different colours
- drama to music from Les Ballets Africains
- learning dance steps
- use of the theatre which is on the same site.

Future plans, if additional funding can be secured, include African drumming and story telling.

Gillian says: 'We are working first and foremost as a group of black people together. People usually say "Oh, it's just for black students, is it?", so you have to be prepared to explain why so that the person goes away with a positive answer…It's targeting groups that have perhaps been marginalised, like women's groups.' Gillian feels that the group helps people to 'acknowledge their culture and backgrounds and to feel comfortable with them. It provides a setting whereby people feel proud of themselves.'

The group is small, with four to six students. Recruitment has been difficult, with a lot of inter-agency liaison. As Gillian says: 'If I depend on one agency, it does not work.' There are close links with Social Services.

Gillian believes passionately in what she is doing. She says: 'These people have been institutionalised, deprived and isolated socially and culturally. They deserve the quality and richness of education.' Gillian says that her work is a drop in the ocean and that more black tutors and more courses are needed, backed up by training, networking and resources.

The Asian Studies course at South Nottinghamshire College

'It's important (to learn about India) because me and my sister haven't been to India before to have a look around…I've seen video, films, but that's it. My mum and dad said they might take us in November'
(Student on the Asian Studies course)

This course was set up in response to a number of Asian students with learning difficulties enrolling at the college. By coincidence, the college recently appointed an Asian principal. The course touches upon 'basics of culture and the countries'. There are twelve students, of whom three are white. The students in the group are a mixture of Muslim, Hindu, Christian and Catholic. Students come from India and Pakistan and Britain.

The course is co-tutored by Roger Banner, a college team leader, and Gurjeet Basi, a community development worker from the India Centre. Gurjeet says: 'Rather than segregation, it's more about being together...the course gives Asian students something to relate to and white students something to learn about.' Topics studied on the course have included the following:

- family trees
- shopping for and cooking Asian food
- looking at the geography of India and Pakistan
- learning words in four languages from Asia – Hindi, Urdu, Gujarati and Bengali
- a practical demonstration of MEHNDIP (decoration of hands with henna)
- looking at different kinds of dress.
- students have brought in their own videos of weddings in their families (one student brought in his own wedding video), and also bring in own tapes of music
- looking at different festivals – such as Diwali.

The course is accredited at entry level by the local Open College Network provider, NEMAP. Course costs and the college tutor costs are funded by FEFC, while Gurjeet works for a voluntary organisation supported by the council. The Equal Opportunities Development Team at the college has been very supportive of the course. The course is planned to continue, although fewer Asian students are predicted for the following year.

The Asian Women's Group at Lambeth Accord

> People liked: 'learning English', 'cooking', 'drawing', 'music', 'dancing' and 'massage'.
>
> People didn't like: 'being interrupted', 'being too rushed', 'men in the kitchen', or 'being told what to do'.
>
> (Members of the Asian Women's group)

Lambeth Accord is a voluntary organisation with a long tradition of fostering self-advocacy work. The Asian Women's group was set up with joint finance after a period of outreach work, when Lipi Begum, the Asian group worker, visited families of potential members. A group for Asian workers was set up to offer advice and guidance on the work.

Leaflets in six languages were sent out: Bengali, Gujarati, Punjabi, Urdu, Hindi and English. They were distributed very widely to Health Centres, doctors' surgeries, libraries and learning difficulties services. The leaflets had to define the term 'learning difficulties' as many people thought it meant someone who needed to learn English or people with mental health problems. These potential misunderstandings are common in translation between languages. For example in Vietnamese, 'carer' means paid worker. It is crucial to have someone who speaks the language and understands the issues involved to check the language.

Most contacts for the group came through Social Services and Community Health services, while some individuals had seen the leaflets. The response was slow and Lambeth Accord had to give a lot of encouragement. They started with an Open Day. Families, workers from Asian community groups and the head of Learning Difficulties services all attended. It was important for the families to meet the group workers and see the venue where the group would meet. The feeling at the meeting was that it would be better to have a women's group as women may have been excluded from a mixed group (people perceive that it is more usual for Asian men to use services than Asian women). Lipi Begum says: 'I had to go and tell the parents what the group was about, they have to trust where they are sending their people. They feel very strongly especially with women with learning difficulties, that they don't want them to go anywhere...We talk about things that happen at home which they can't talk about elsewhere. It reminds them of their culture, we talk in the language that they want to talk.' Bengali and Gujarati are both spoken in the group. One woman said through an interpreter: 'I want to meet people who speak Gujarati.' She was keen to learn English at the Brixton Centre but did not want to use a bus.

Activities have included:

- Celebrating festivals such as Diwali
- Basic English language work, looking at different words, for instance one week different pieces of fruit which were felt and tasted. Two of the women in the group are blind and they enjoyed this
- Hand massage and hand painting
- Listening and dancing to Asian music
- Talking about religion, fasts and what has been happening.

Although this provision is organised by Lambeth Accord rather than a continuing education provider, the extensive outreach work and emphasis on use of mother tongue for students, combined with the range of culturally-appropriate learning opportunities, could well provide a useful model for education to follow.

Diversity and ethnic origins

Celebrating diversity and valuing ethnic origins also matters for other groups, such as Jewish or Welsh people with learning dificulties. We heard of one case where a speech therapist assessed a man with learning difficulties in English. The man's first language was in fact Welsh, and a very misleading picture of his communication skills was given. Similarly, a man with learning difficulties in a long-stay hospital was described as going around muttering gibberish. In fact he was reciting snatches of Hebrew prayers, but nobody had realised until a Jewish visitor picked up on this. One colleague, the principal of an inner city sixth-form college, has found that some students from minority ethnic groups who have difficulty in speaking English have been wrongly labelled as having learning difficulties. Access to English for Speakers of Other Languages (ESOL) classes for people with learning difficulties is also an issue: we found very few examples of this in our trawl for information.

Provision for Welsh speakers with learning difficulties in North Wales

'If I had to speak English, I'd never be able to say what is bothering me…'
(Welsh speaker with learning difficulties)

'We live and work in a bilingual community and both English and Welsh have equal status in the college.'
(Coleg Menai)

'Giving a person real choice regarding use of language is the essence of good practice – denying their rights is a way of oppressing that person.'
(CCETSW in Wales)

The Welsh Language Act (1993) requires the use of written and spoken Welsh to be available to people whose first language is Welsh. Coleg Menai is in Gwynedd, North Wales, which is a strong Welsh-speaking area. The college therefore offers tuition for people with learning difficulties in both English and Welsh. Gwynedd has had a bilingual policy since 1974. All of the teaching and learning is offered on a bilingual basis. About 80 percent of the students with learning difficulties speak Welsh as a first language. A similar number of teaching and support staff are fluent in Welsh. Staff who don't speak Welsh are offered the opportunity to learn it. One difficulty is that few teaching resources are available in Welsh and most need translating. The college has identified a need for a basic skills assessment to be available in Welsh. The college has the back-up of two full-time translators to help prepare materials across the college. As one tutor commented about teaching in Welsh: 'Round here, you just do it!' Another made the point that: 'It's natural in Gwynedd, which might not be the case elsewhere in Wales.'

Gender issues for adults with learning difficulties

The case study from Lambeth Accord earlier in this chapter gives insights into specialist provision for a group of Asian women with learning difficulties. We know from *Mapping Provision* that women with learning difficulties are slightly under-represented in the student population. What initiatives have there been to offer gender-specific learning opportunities?

Groups for women...and men too

At the College of North East London, Paul Craven explains why he helped to set up separate groups for men and women with learning difficulties in 1991: 'I have been in touch with the disability world a long time through teaching people with learning difficulties and disabilities and I became acutely aware that people in general had very few opportunities to explore sensitive issues in a private way.'

Paul felt that a lot of women with learning difficulties didn't know about issues such as sexuality and periods, because they were not told about things. Everyday things such as greeting

> 'There are some things that women want to talk about on their own.'
> (Member of the women's group at the College of North East London)
>
> 'With women I can talk about different things…I don't have to be embarrassed with men not here.'
>
> 'We support and help each other'
> (Members of the women's group at Clarendon College)
>
> 'More on women's issues!'
> (Evaluation by woman who attended health workshop at Brighton University)

people and learning how to listen to others were skills that many people also needed an opportunity to develop. As communication skills are an important part of the work, the English Speaking Board Certificate in Communication is studied, which is relevant to the learners' needs. The course is funded by the FEFC and has a woman tutor. There is a men's group along similar lines, talking about difficult issues.

Clarendon College also has a long-established women's group. They have recently followed an Open College Network accredited course on 'Advocacy and citizenship'. Amongst other topics, they have studied women's votes and the suffragettes and looked at rights and responsibilities.

The Centre for Continuing Education at the University of Sussex has run separate one-day workshop sessions on men's health and women's health. A facilitator and a practice nurse worked together to answer queries about health, which ranged from periods to sunburn and mental health. Kathy Smith of the University commented that learning about the menopause seems not to have been addressed for older women with learning difficulties. There may be scope for a course for older women to talk about the menopause and about the various changes that occur.

One user-led course is run by Skills for People, a voluntary organisation in Newcastle upon Tyne, where a course is planned and presented by women with learning difficulties, with some visiting speakers. Women's health, rights and self-defence are a few of the topics covered.

Making choices about accessing the community and using transport – a course for women

'We talk about it.'

'We plan it.'

'How are we going to get there?'

'The money for the trip.'

(Women from the Community Day course)

In Manchester, it was noticed that although more women with learning difficulties took part in learning, they were less likely to progress through the adult education service than men. Brenda Buttery says that: 'There was an under-representation of women moving through.' She surveyed a number of women by questionnaire and interview, to talk the questions through. Brenda found that their chances to make choices were very limited, with parents or carers taking a lead role. For this reason, the 'Community Day' was developed. The course aims to help women access the community while developing decision-making skills. The emphasis is on women making their own choices. The course runs for five hours a week over two years, and is accredited by the Greater Manchester Open College Federation.

Learning activities have included:

- Using a variety of transport: buses, Metro
- Learning to travel independently to/from the class
- Joining in with International Women's Day taster courses
- Planning a coffee morning to fund-raise for the Down's Syndrome Association
- Going to a women's day at a pool for International Women's Day.

My favourite was the one with the bubbles...Jacuzzi...at first I was a bit frightened, but then I thought it was really good, I liked it.'

The women say they like the group because:
- 'It's helped me.'
- 'You can talk openly.'
- 'You can talk about women's matters.'

Working with older learners

The book *Fair Shares for All?* looks at disparities in provision, including access to services for older adults with learning difficulties. The findings were depressing. Support staff were cautious about the ability of older adults with learning difficulties to acquire new skills, so much so that 30 percent of staff did not see training as of relevance for people over 60. The authors write: 'In addition, the group had less favourable access to further education colleges – one respondent, for example, was refused a place because he was too old...' Few people with learning difficulties over 60 were accessing education. Walker, Ryan and Walker describe how falling between services for older people and services for people with learning difficulties

leaves older people with learning difficulties 'even more excluded and marginalised' and facing a 'double jeopardy'.

The Open University has recognised that the histories of
people with learning difficulties who lived in long-stay hospitals were in danger of being lost and forgotten. Conferences on
oral history have been held, and the book *Forgotten Lives*
includes stories from people with learning difficulties and photographs. Few examples of specific educational provision for
older learners were given to NIACE for the project *All Things
Being Equal?* We describe below one positive example of provision for older adults with learning difficulties, which draws on
reminiscence work with a group of learners who all lived in
long-stay hospitals for much of their lives.

Crafting our Memories

'This is training, isn't it? Training is good!'

'I like angels. Religious things. I like drawing angels. Stained glass
windows.'

'My first memory is going to the shops with my mum...'

(Students from the 'Crafting our Memories' group)

'Crafting our Memories' offers a chance for older adults with
learning difficulties to share their memories together. All of the
people in the group have spent years in two long-stay hospitals
before moving to live in Southwark. The class is the result of
collaboration between Southwark Education Older Learners'
Project and an arts organisation called Entelechy. It is part of a
three-year research and development programme called 'Redis-
covering our Histories', which is supported by the Department
of Health. The publicity invites learners to:

'Come and share your memories. Remember places where you have lived; things you have seen and done. Words are not important. We will use paint, paste, paper and many other bits and pieces to make and create things...Pictures and objects that say something about ourselves; stories we can show and share with others.'

There are six students in the group. The levels of support are good, with one tutor and three volunteers, plus a support worker from another agency. This means that a lot of the work can be done one-to-one. The group have made their own individual memory books with words and drawings. One student talked about the gardening he used to do and drew pictures. The tutor wrote down the story he told about his memories of gardening next to the pictures. The student then started making models of the various tools he used in the garden out of salt dough. Sometimes the memories which come up are unpleasant, so a supportive atmosphere is essential. Future plans include inviting non-disabled older adults to join the group and perhaps making links with South Bank University.

▶ Summary

Few places yet provide courses for adults with learning difficulties which are specifically tailored for race, gender and age. The case studies which we found were comparatively rare.

There is a dearth of access routes to learning for under-represented groups of adults with learning difficulties, while the absence of such learners is not even recognised in many places.

Students valued the chance to meet in same-race, -gender or -age groups.

Outreach work and inter-agency work were common to a

number of the examples, for example liaison with community groups, parents and Social Services.

Producing publicity in relevant languages and providing bilingual staff was crucial in setting up both the Asian Women's group at Lambeth Accord and the bilingual provision at Coleg Menai.

Making it happen – a checklist of ideas

▶ Which potential learners are missing from your service?

▶ Which groups of adults with learning difficulties are represented in the community but not in your education classes?

▶ Is there specific provision in your area which caters, where relevant, for:
- adults with learning difficulties from black, Asian, Chinese or other minority ethnic groups?
- men with learning difficulties?
- women with learning difficulties?
- older adults with learning difficulties?
- Welsh speakers with learning difficulties?
- Jewish people with learning difficulties?

If not:

- how would you prioritise developments?
- what steps could you take to establish relevant provision?
- how can you provide access routes into continuing education?
- what partners could you work with?
- what funding sources could you access?

REFERENCES/RESOURCES

Chris Hatton, Sabiha Azmi, Eric Emerson and Amanda Caine, *Improving services for South Asian adults with learning difficulties* (RNIB *Focus* newsletter, Number 22, October 1997)

Black People First Conference Report (1994, People First)

Carol Walker, Tony Ryan and Alan Walker, *Fair Shares for All?* (1996, Pavilion Publishing in association with the Joseph Rowntree Foundation)

Dorothy Atkinson, Mark Jackson and Jan Walmsley (eds), *Forgotten Lives: Exploring the history of learning disability* (1997, British Institute of Learning Disabilities)

Jane Lewis *Give Us a Voice* (1996, Choice Press)

Looking Back, Looking Forward Reminiscence with people with learning disabilities. Developed by Mary Stuart (1997, Pavillion Publishing)

Mapping Provision (1997, FEFC)

Resources for women with learning difficulties

No Means No, Group safety video by Walsall Women's Group (Pavilion Publishing, Brighton)

Women First A book by women with learning difficulties about the issues for women with learning difficulties (People First supported by Camden and Islington Health Authority)

A book is planned which is a collaboration between women with and without learning difficulties. Enquiries to:

Dorothy Atkinson
Department of Health and Social Welfare
Open University
Walton Hall
Milton Keynes MK7 6AA

5

Tailoring the curriculum: disability and difference

The previous chapter looked at race, ethnicity, gender and age in relation to education for adults with learning difficulties. This chapter looks at provision which caters for adults with learning difficulties who:

- have profound and multiple learning difficulties
- have been labelled as presenting challenging behaviour
- have additional mental health difficulties
- have additional sensory impairments or disabilities.

Adults with profound/multiple learning difficulties

Education for adults with profound and multiple learning difficulties does exist, but is very patchy nationally. What are the main issues?

Securing funding

Some Local Education Authorities offer provision for this group of learners, with one or two offering a number of courses. At the time of writing, the Further Education Funding Council (FEFC) is actively considering the implementation of the recommendations from the *Inclusive Learning* report. One of the recommendations relates to the expansion of opportunities for adults with

profound and multiple learning difficulties. The current constraints of demonstrating progression for FEFC funding have
generally inhibited developments in provision for this group of
potential learners, although they are not excluded. However,
widening participation will inevitably have cost implications
for colleges and LEAs.

Physical access is a barrier

Many places are still physically inaccessible for students with
profound and multiple learning difficulties, who may use
wheelchairs or require changing facilities.

There will be more adults with profound and multiple learning difficulties in the future

It is predicted that the numbers of adults with profound and
multiple learning difficulties will rise, as more babies and
young children who have very severe disabilities are surviving
into adulthood, due to improved medical care.

How far has care in the community come?

We noticed that several places offer educational provision on
the sites of long-stay hospitals. In some cases, people have left
hospital to live in the community... and are then bussed back to
the same hospital for their education. Perhaps this is just
where the facilities happen to be, but it offers a very segregated
experience for the learners. It may also deny the opportunity to
put this life in the past – as a history – and to move on.

Ideas about quality and what should be learnt vary enormously

In some cases, provision is relatively new. In others, it has been
established for a number of years. Hospitals and day centres
can be in quite remote places, and practitioners can be physically quite isolated. There was a huge divergence in approaches

used to teach students with profound and multiple learning difficulties, possibly because of the relative isolation and perhaps because quality standards are still emerging. Provision ranged from a college which included people with profound and multiple learning difficulties in ordinary vocational classes with one-to-one support, through to adult education classes where the focus was on fine motor skills and communication skills in closed groups. There is scope for further research and development to explore some of these issues in greater depth than is possible here.

Provision at Hertford Regional College

Hertford Regional College offers three full-time two-year courses for adults with profound and multiple learning difficulties. The work is underpinned by inter-agency co-operation. Staffing and premises are shared with Social Services. As Ian Harris, who manages the work for the college, comments: 'In order to deliver effectively, we need to work alongside Social Services.' There is close liaison and joint planning, while shared training and regular meetings are also essential. Some courses are run at college, while others are offered at a day centre. Courses in art, music and other subjects are taught by subject specialists, with back-up from support workers. Lecturers and day service social workers work in partnership. The shared approach includes classroom delivery, reviewing progress and planning for the next step. In one class visited, a vocalisation by a man with profound learning difficulties had been recorded and dubbed against a rhythmic soundtrack. He clearly recognised his own voice, set to music, and responded positively to it.

Mr Evans, the college principal, is wholeheartedly supportive of the provision. At lunch during the project visit, he was visibly relaxed and comfortable with the students, joking with them and wiping chins as needed. He has accompanied the students on trips out and occasionally joins them at lunch times. He sees the work as protecting the interests of the most vulnerable learners in the college.

When the Further and Higher Education Act (1992) was implemented, college senior managers were determined to understand how best to obtain FEFC funding for people with severe disabilities. They took a profoundly disabled young woman as an example, to see how funding could be obtained. Two college lecturers were given three weeks' remission from teaching duties to investigate how to apply for funding at about the time that the FHE Act (1992) funding changes were introduced. Consideration is currently being given to accreditation of learning *via* the Unit Award Scheme operated by the Northern Examinations and Assessment Board (NEAB).

Speaking Without Words at Skills For People

Skills For People, a voluntary organisation in Newcastle upon Tyne, felt that people with learning difficulties who do not use words were being left out of their courses. They developed Speaking Without Words, a five-week course for people with profound and multiple learning difficulties who do not use words. The planning team for the course consisted of two women with learning difficulties who do not use words, their support workers and two staff from Skills For People.

The course starts with an introductory session just for staff/carers to introduce them to the theory of the course. Aletta Seymour, the course organiser, explains how the course works:

'Everyone comes along with a carer of their choice who they work with throughout the course…it is a chance to learn together…The sessions give people the chance to spend time together thinking about how we communicate in ways other than words…Everything people do is a communication, if people communicate they feel better about themselves.'

The course looks at the five senses. There are music, art and reflexology sessions. Body work is seen to be important as some people with profound and multiple learning difficulties often only have their bodies touched for personal care needs and do not have a chance to enjoy their bodies. In some sessions the group do things like asking the staff not to talk for a period.

The activities on the course are based on work in Phoebe Caldwell's book *Getting In Touch* and a VIA publication *Face to Face* by Bill Puddicombe. Skills For People hope that staff go away and put some of the things learned on the course into practice. There is an ongoing support group for people who have done the course.

Provision for people with learning difficulties who have been labelled as presenting challenging behaviour

'Our aim is that all our clients access college.'

'Our clients can display the worst of challenging behaviour. It [college] is a completely new venture for us and our clients…we are very encouraged from the feedback from staff and students.'

(Quotes from Health Authority staff)

Challenging behaviour has been defined by a team at the University of Kent as 'behaviour of such an intensity, frequency or duration that the physical safety of the person or others is likely to be placed in serious jeopardy, or behaviour which is likely to seriously limit or delay access to and use of ordinary community facilities.'

Solihull College is committed to welcoming students with learning difficulties who also present challenging behaviour. The college picked up on the under-representation of this group from the *Inclusive Learning* report, and decided to take positive action. As Vicky Lowe, Manager for Students with Additional

Needs, put it: 'Tomlinson gave us an opportunity to stand back and look at what we were doing and who with…the college had worked with these groups before but Tomlinson made us refocus our attention.'

Working with other agencies was a crucial part of the college's strategy in supporting students with learning difficulties who have challenging behaviour.

The college works on the basis that it is best to talk to agencies before the student comes to college and give them clear boundaries about what the college will accept. For example, if the student can be violent, the support must be set up carefully and should be available at all times. It is a problem when the support workers are different each week and there is no consistency. If considering support staff from the college team, they look at the strengths of individual staff. They look for a colleague who is mature and experienced in order to provide good support for a student with challenging behaviour.

Factors which have helped the work at Solihull College to succeed include the following:

- The importance of a good relationship between the college and the referral agencies.
- Consistency in the support workers who support students in their classes.
- Good quality support so that students feel part of the whole group.
- Class tutors feeling well supported by the staff from the Learning Support team.
- Thorough assessment of the students' support needs before they start a class.

Sue Hatton, the co-ordinator of part-time provision at the college for adults with learning difficulties, does an initial assessment. Each person is taken as an individual with varying needs. Sue says: 'The question is really, have we got provision for this person that will best support their needs and have we got a good relationship with the agency?"

Provision for people with learning difficulties and additional mental health difficulties

'Hopefully I will get a lot more confident and do a lot more things next year…'

(Student with both learning difficulties and mental health difficulties)

Adults with the dual impairment of learning difficulties and mental health difficulties often fall between the two services and can miss out educationally. Several colleges told us that in recent years the incidence of young adults with both learning difficulties and behavioural problems had increased.

Hackney Community College

Janice Ferguson and Rosita Matyniowna work with students with learning difficulties at Hackney Community College. Many of their students also have mental health problems. Students come to college aged 18 or 19, having had the learning difficulties label all of their lives. If a student has mental health problems, they often seem to have been overlooked and the resulting behaviour is put down to their learning difficulties.

Janice and Rosita have found that most of the students with learning difficulties who also have mental health problems have been abused physically, mentally, or sexually, and in some cases all of these. The college encourages students to learn to speak up for themselves and it is often at this stage that students disclose to staff about their abuse.

It is clear that people with learning difficulties have a right to sex education, and to have the opportunity to discuss what behaviour from other people is acceptable or not. However, being informed about sexuality does not in itself prevent the misuse of power that is implicit in sexual abuse.

- Sara has learning difficulties and attended the school leavers' course at the college. She had wild mood swings and could sometimes be violent. It transpired that she was regularly being abused by her step-father. This came to a crisis point one day when Sara came into college and told the staff that her step-father had raped her. As a consequence of this crisis and the aftermath, she was reassessed and found to be schizophrenic. She had up until that point always received learning difficulties services.

- Wendy is a student on the Vocational Preparation course. She has moderate learning difficulties and mental health problems and experiences panic attacks. She had 'bunked off' school a lot because of this. Wendy's behaviour meant that she was constantly not finishing courses and sabotaged anything she did manage to achieve. Janice worked out a strategy with her. When Wendy felt stressed, they agreed that she could leave the room to go out and get some air or a cup of tea. Janice would check that she was all right at the end of class. Wendy has completed a year at college and is going on to a GNVQ course.

- One student with learning difficulties and mental health problems is employed part-time by the college as a self-advocacy support worker. She works with a tutor running a self-advocacy class and sometimes takes a lead role. This student is about to do her Initial Teacher Training course.

Janice and Rosita feel that when working with students with learning difficulties who have mental health problems, it is important to:

- work together with other agencies, such as the Social Services Learning Difficulties team and Health Trusts
- have access to staff with basic counselling skills
- have support from managers
- have knowledge about funding

- network with other colleges
- try and get mental health on the organisation's agenda – for example, inclusion in disability statements.

Provision for adults with learning difficulties who have additional sensory impairments

'I have just started to read Braille, I have to practise every night.'
(Blind man with learning difficulties)

'I feel I would like to be the same as anybody else. Because I have a dual disability, I have been left out of the deaf community.'
(Deaf man with learning difficulties)

People with learning difficulties and an additional sensory disability can miss out on learning. It is estimated that 40 per cent of adults with learning difficulties have a problem with their eyesight or hearing. There is also a substantive overlap between sight and hearing loss. These difficulties often go undetected. The RNIB has a useful set of leaflets available for staff about both eye-sight and hearing.

A few places are offering provision for deaf or blind students with learning difficulties. Keith Dalgleish, a worker at CHANGE who is blind, told us about his cookery class:

'I go to Cook and Eat at East Ham, this is my second year. There are two people running it, Stella and Mary. It is every Friday 10-2. Last week we made a list and I had to go out and get my own shopping. Then we made our own toasted sandwich. I go by taxi. When I started I had a support worker but I wanted to be independent and on my own. They have special stuff, equipment. There is an opener for tins and a peeler, a little knife, a folding up chopping board and talking scales that tell you how many ounces of flour you need for dough. In the cookery class they tell us what we have to do and we have notes in our folders. There is a special cooker. I want to learn to cook for myself. The place where I live now [a large hostel] will be shutting in two years' time and we will be moving into the community."

Learning Support: a course for deaf adults with learning difficulties in Manchester

'We learn sign and the teachers learn sign as well...'

'We are all the same.'

(Deaf students with learning difficulties)

This course is attended by eight students with learning difficulties who are deaf or partially hearing. It is FEFC-funded and is also accredited by the Greater Manchester Open College Federation. The syllabus includes sign language and deaf awareness, as well as basic skills, cookery, art and health issues. The students are referred from a number of organisations within Greater Manchester. The course used to be taught by hearing tutors, but is now taught by deaf tutors. This has made an important difference. As Judith Kidd, the lead tutor, explains: 'We know our own culture. Hearing tutors don't know. They haven't had the experience of deaf culture. There can be a real inequality there...'

▶ Summary

Provision for the learners described in this chapter is very patchy nationally. The examples of practice which we found were relatively rare.

Expanding opportunities for adults with profound and multiple learning difficulties is a recommendation of the *Inclusive Learning* report, which is under consideration by the Further Education Funding Council at the time of writing.

Some colleges, such as Solihull College and Hertford Regional College, had made a strategic decision to work with under-represented groups: those with challenging behaviour and those with profound and multiple learning difficulties respectively.

An estimated 40 per cent of people with learning difficulties have an additional difficulty with sight or hearing. These difficulties can often go undetected and appropriate support and provision for them is not readily available.

Making it happen – a checklist of ideas

▶ What links do you have with social services, health, voluntary organisations and other agencies?

▶ Is there a budget for adaptations or specialist equipment?

▶ Are there learning opportunities in your area which cater for adults with learning difficulties who:
- have profound and multiple learning difficulties?
- have been labelled as presenting challenging behaviour?
- have additional mental health difficulties?
- have additional sensory impairments or disabilities?

If not:

- what steps could you take to create opportunities?
- what partners could you work with?
- what would the resource implications be?

RESOURCES

Phoebe Caldwell, *Getting in Touch: Ways of working with people with severe learning difficulties and extensive support needs* (1996, Pavilion Publishing/ Joseph Rowntree Foundation)

Learning for Life A pack to support learning opportunities for adults who have profound intellectual and multiple physical disabilities (1994, FEDA: now out of print)

Bill Puddicombe, *Face to Face* (About communicating without language) (1995, VIA)

Melanie Nind and Dave Hewitt, *Access to Communication* (1994, David Fulton Publications)

Melanie Nind and Dave Hewitt, *Interaction in action* (1998, David Fulton Publications)

Ain't Misbehavin': Positive approaches to disruptive behaviour (1998, FEDA)

Leaflets from RNIB include:

- Looking for eye problems in people with learning difficulties
- Hints on teaching people with visual and learning difficulties
- Looking for hearing problems in people with learning difficulties
- Improving environments for people with visual and learning disabilities

The MAP Pack – More Access Please Accessible information pack about people with learning difficulties and sensory disabilities (1997, CHANGE)

6

Support

Support is provided in a variety of forms both for marginalised groups of students with learning difficulties and the staff who work with them. This chapter looks at the different ways in which support is being provided and developed in continuing education.

Support for the student

Students with learning difficulties from marginalised groups may need one-to-one support when they attend their classes. Staff from Social Services day centres and residential support workers frequently accompany people with learning difficulties to and into their college or adult education classes.

In FE colleges support may be provided by in-house staff from the Learning Support Team. These staff may be known, for example, as education support workers, inclusive education officers or learning assistants.

The role of the support worker is a complex one. This is often not acknowledged and consequently the role can be undervalued, particularly for support staff from outside agencies.

Support workers play a key role in the learning situation and it is important that the help which the support worker offers is positive and focused. Some colleges and adult education services provide training and guidelines for support workers. This subject is covered in more detail in Chapter 8.

The consistency and quality of support workers from external agencies was a cause of concern for several education staff who were interviewed as part of the fieldwork visits for this project. Indeed at one college an inspection had identified poor support from external support workers as an issue that needed to be addressed.

Consistency

It can be extremely difficult for a productive learning partnership to develop if, each week, a student finds themselves working with a different support worker in class. Having some consistency in the support role, with one or two support workers who take it in turns to support an individual in class, ensures that a working relationship can develop between:

- the student and the support worker
- the support worker and the class tutor
- the support worker and the other students in the class.

One tutor commented:

'The fact is that if it is the same person (support worker), there is continuity and it makes it easier...I think that it's very important, that's helped me build confidence, because Anne is there as support for Bill, but she is also there as support for me.'

The student themselves will feel more confident working with a worker they know and who is also familiar with the class. Continuity of support will lead to continuity in learning for the student. It will avoid the tutor having to explain repeatedly to different support workers the details of their role in class, taking precious time and attention away from the student.

In a cookery class which was visited for the project, a support worker had accompanied two students to almost all of the sessions of the class. The support worker was very much a part of the whole group. It was difficult to tell whom she was accompanying as the students, although relatively new to the group, were fully integrated.

Consistency can bring a sense of job satisfaction for the support workers themselves. As they work with a student over a period of time, it is possible to observe how the student develops and progresses in their learning.

Quality support for students

The City of Liverpool Community College is one of several colleges that has a team of trained and experienced support staff who give one-to-one support to students with learning difficulties in a range of mainstream and discrete classes.

A student with learning difficulties who does not speak has been supported in a mainstream Woodcraft/Carpentry class where he has produced a beautiful casement clock. His support worker described her role:

> '…I'm part of the class. I don't just want to be known as Bill's support worker. I interact with everybody else as well…I think it has helped Bill be more accepted in the group as well, in his own right.'

Students value the help they receive

- An older woman with learning difficulties, talking about her support worker who works with her on a one-to-one basis in a literacy class, explained that:

  'It would be hard without her if I was on my own, because I didn't learn a lot at school. I never tried learning on my own, I need a bit more help.'

Tutorials

Tutorial support on a one-to-one basis is provided in some places as part of a learning support 'package' to students with learning difficulties.

- At Blackburn College, for example, a deaf man with learning difficulties on a car maintenance course has a one-to-one supported study session for two hours a week. He meets with his personal tutor to go over notes or to discuss any issues or problems that might have come up in his classes during the week.
- A lecturer working with students with learning difficulties and mental health problems offers the students tutorials where:
  '...the disability side is not emphasised, We look at what they can do to build their self-esteem and confidence, then we move on from there.'

Volunteers

Volunteers can play a role in supporting students with learning difficulties from marginalised groups to access continuing education.

A reminiscence group, for older people with learning difficulties who have been institutionalised, meets in a neighbourhood centre. A local resident volunteers as a support worker in the group.

Some areas have well established volunteer schemes:
- The Linking Scheme run by Dorset County Council links students with learning difficulties with volunteers who support them in mainstream classes. One volunteer who supports a women with learning difficulties commented that the student:
  '... mixes well with the class and is now able to play a game of badminton with other members – and I can too.'

Support out of class

Support for access

Students with learning difficulties from marginalised groups often need support in travelling to a class. Good liaison between education staff and the support staff who will be working with the student is essential. An organiser of a group for older people with learning difficulties stressed the importance of liaising with support workers:

> '...the better the relationship, the better the access for the student.'

A worker with the same group made the point that:

> 'Transport to and from the group is a major issue...On occasion, especially near the beginning of the group, weekly contact prior to the meeting was necessary to remind support staff that the activity was taking place, and transport needed to be arranged.'

Support for student life

Students with learning difficulties from marginalised groups may need support to use college facilities such as the library and canteen, and have the opportunity to mix with other students:

- An inclusive education officer talked about her support 'fading out' when appropriate, to enable a student to get on with tasks or be with people independently, especially during break times.

At Solihull College, during the first class of the year, the students and support workers spend some time finding their way around the college facilities with a guide provided by the tutor.

Support for choice and learning

Supporting students to choose which course they want to do is an important initial step which can be difficult for many students with learning difficulties. WORKOUT, a voluntary organisation based in Eastbourne, supports people with learning difficulties and mental health problems who want to go to college. Staff support individuals by:

- going through the course information with them
- helping complete application forms
- supporting individuals at interview
- providing regular reviews during the course.

Peer support

In Derbyshire, adults with learning difficulties have trained to teach Makaton skills to other people with learning difficulties who have communication difficulties.

Specialist equipment and facilities

Marginalised groups of students with learning difficulties who have additional or complex needs may need particular equipment or facilities to help them with their learning.

- A blind student with learning difficulties uses a set of talking scales in his adult education cookery class.
- In one college, staff working with students with learning difficulties and challenging behaviour have a changing room available for staff to help students with personal care needs. There is also a room for staff and students to be alone at

times during the day when they need space. A Muslim student is able to use this room to pray in, and having this facility has made a real difference to how he copes with his day at college.

Adaptations need not be costly or difficult:

- A deaf student with learning difficulties who also has Usher's syndrome found it hard to read writing which was on a white background. Her tutor stopped using a whiteboard. Notes for the student were provided on coloured paper to make them easier for her to read.
- An older woman with learning difficulties who has full use of only one of her hands attends a dressmaking class. Certain pieces of equipment are being adapted for the student, e.g. a frame to hold material for tacking and some curved needles.

Specialist skills

Specialist skills, such as sign language, are used when working with some marginalised groups of students with learning difficulties. However, the specific needs of the students must be recognised and the skills need to be adapted accordingly.

Richard West, who is a deaf man with learning difficulties, pointed out that:

> '… people with learning difficulties who are deaf need more support than people with hearing. Sometimes it is difficult to understand British Sign Language because the words are not clear and sometimes it may not have been taught at school. You can use different ways of talking to a person, showing words and photographs to choose so they can say what it means.'

One FE college has started to provide classes for autistic students who live in homes run by the National Autistic Society (NAS). The college is contracting NAS staff in, to support students in college because of their particular expertise. The manager responsible for this commented:

> *'It is important here to have multi-disciplinary work as FE can't meet all the needs.'*

At Hertfordshire Regional College, physiotherapists and speech therapists have given specialist inputs to courses for students with profound and multiple learning difficulties.

Support for tutors

Isolation

Lecturers and tutors working with students with learning difficulties from marginalised groups often feel isolated themselves:

- A lecturer working with people with learning difficulties and mental health problems in an off-site location said she had a feeling of 'not belonging'. She made the point that perhaps this feeling was similar to how some of the students she worked with felt. She remarked that in continuing education:
  '...the needs of my students and us as staff are not recognised.'

In recognition of these issues, three network meetings for staff working in continuing education with people with learning difficulties were arranged as part of the *All Things Being Equal?* project. One participant commented:

> *'...I feel that giving people a space and some quality time to discuss issues affecting them with others encountering the same difficulties was the most valuable experience...'*

Tutor support systems

Support for tutors can be part of a formal support system or it can be available on a less formal basis. Some FE colleges have set up a framework of support across college in their Learning Support Teams. At Solihull College, as well as help from the Learning Assistant who works with the student in the sessions, class tutors are supported by Support Tutors from the Learning Support Team. Their responsibilities include:

* assessing the student's additional needs
* being a contact person for subject tutors
* liaising with external agencies
* adapting class materials if necessary
* supporting students in lessons if required.

If a new student who has particular support needs, for example due to challenging behaviour, joins a class the lecturer meets with the tutor to discuss the support arrangements beforehand.

An adult education tutor working with students with profound and multiple learning difficulties felt well supported by the lecturer in charge, as the lecturer:

* made a point of visiting the class regularly
* was easy to contact
* would make time to arrange to meet, to listen to and discuss any problems or questions the tutor might have.

Support from senior managers

Working with students with learning difficulties from marginalised groups can be regarded as a bit risky or different and is sometimes questioned or criticised by other staff. Introducing new courses for students who are not used to being at college takes a lot of time and work. It is therefore crucial when doing this kind of work to have support from senior managers:

* At one college where there is new provision for students with learning difficulties and challenging behaviour, cross-college

awareness sessions have been run for all teaching and non-teaching staff, including senior managers.
- One college working with students with learning difficulties and challenging behaviour has the Vice Principal on its Inclusive Learning steering group. The Vice Principal has also taken time to visit other colleges doing similar work.

▶ Summary

The quality of support which marginalised students receive has a fundamental effect on their whole experience of continuing education.

Continuity of staff is a key issue.

Working with students from marginalised groups with learning difficulties can, in some instances, be an isolating experience for staff. They also need support.

It is important to have the support of senior management.

Making it happen – a checklist of ideas

Student support

What support for students is offered in your organisation:
- getting to class
- at enrolment
- in class
- using general college facilities?

Do you liaise regularly with external referral agencies who provide support for students who come to classes?

Have you offered outside agencies training or joint meetings to discuss the importance and value of consistency and high quality of support for students?

▶ Do you have any written guidelines for support workers about their role?

▶ Is there a need for specialist support for some students?

▶ Do the students have a say in the support they receive?

Support for staff

▶ How are staff working with students with learning difficulties from marginalised groups supported in your organisation? Do you:
- provide training?
- meet regularly with tutors to discuss any issues they may have?
- visit classes regularly?
- give advice on adapting class materials?
- if appropriate, discuss with tutors the needs of individual students before they join a class?

Management support

▶ Are senior management aware of the work you do?

▶ How can you involve them in the development of your work?

▶ Do you invite them to events where they can meet the students and see their work?

RESOURCES

Jeannie Sutcliffe, *Module 8 and 9 of Towards Inclusion – Developing Integrated Education for Adults with Learning Difficulties*, a staff development pack (1996, NIACE)

7

Working together:
the inter-agency dimension

> 'If you depend on one agency, it doesn't work...'
>
> (Adult education development worker)

Working together with other agencies underpins the majority of the provision for adults with learning difficulties from marginalised groups which is described in this book. This chapter considers what partners are involved and what the benefits are, as well as some of the difficulties that can occur.

Who is involved?

We found a range of people working collaboratively. The table opposite gives a brief outline of people's roles and the broad nature of their involvement. This listing is not exhaustive but serves to give a flavour of the partners involved.

Apart from education staff, colleagues from health and social services departments are more likely to be involved than other professionals, but all have a role to play.

People involved	Indication of roles
College staff and LEA adult education staff	Teaching, supporting, guidance, liaison, transport in some cases
School staff	Referring students on to continuing education
Social services staff	In class support, transport, liaison Provision of co-tutors in one or two cases
Health trust/authority residential staff	In class support, transport, liaison
Voluntary organisation staff	In class support, transport, liaison Provision of tutors or co-tutors in a few cases
Physiotherapists	Input for students with profound/ multiple learning difficulties
Speech therapists	Input for students with profound/ multiple learning difficulties
Volunteers	In class support, transport,
Relatives	Targeted for publicity/information
Community groups for black and Asian people	Targeted for publicity/information Source of tutors in one or two cases
Mental health professionals	Called in occasionally when people with learning difficulties have exhibited mental health difficulties
Private companies	A private company works with a college to provide education on site for people with learning difficulties and challenging behaviour

Joint planning

Much of the evidence of the 1996 *Inclusive Learning* report: '...testified to an absence of joint work between social and health services and further education managers.'

The report devotes a whole section to the importance of collaborative working between agencies in improving access to continuing education for students with learning difficulties. The Government's 1998 Green Paper *The Learning Age* also recognises collaborative working as central to widening participation for adults with learning difficulties in continuing education.

Joint planning with social services and health services is very significant when developing education provision for marginalised groups of students with learning difficulties in continuing education. If it is not something that happens in your organisation, it is worth finding out if education has a mention in your local authority's Community Care plan and trying to get it on the agenda.

Some education staff are actively involved in joint planning with colleagues from other agencies. Senior managers work together on policy and funding issues; Heads of Service can plan and liaise together. Tutors and front-line staff from other agencies can work and plan together around individual students' learning needs.

Working with your peers in other organisations you can:

- gain a wider picture of any unmet needs for groups of marginalised people with learning difficulties in your area
- where appropriate, explore ways to develop provision and share expertise to meet these needs.

What are the benefits of working together?

There are a number of benefits in working together. Resources, staffing and training can be shared. In most cases, the provision for marginalised groups which we saw was built on partnerships. This included:

- social workers and a college tutor co-delivering a course for deaf adults with learning difficulties
- a black arts development worker working with Social Services and local community groups to get referrals for black students with learning difficulties
- courses for people with profound and multiple learning difficulties being jointly resourced, planned and staffed by a college and Social Services
- a course for older learners with learning difficulties being run as a collaboration between a voluntary arts group and an LEA adult education programme.

Allowing staff adequate time for liaison is important. One London borough's Adult Education Service with a long tradition of multi-agency work recently merged with a college. Time to attend inter-agency meetings has been drastically cut back. The staff involved are concerned that the long-term future of the work will suffer, as joint planning and joint funding no longer have priority.

Good communication is important so that values, roles and responsibilities can be effectively shared. People generally felt that collaboration at the top, with the involvement of senior managers, was supportive and helpful in taking forward 'grass roots' work.

What are the difficulties?

There can be difficulties in partnership work. Sometimes planning cycles in different agencies vary, which can make it hard to dovetail joint planning and resourcing. Sometimes the priorities of staff and organisations differ. For example, a group home may free a different staff member each week on a rota basis to accompany a person to college. For the college or adult education tutor, having the same member of staff attending every week is often essential for continuity.

The language and terminology used by different agencies, such as 'challenging behaviour', can mean different things in different contexts, which can be a barrier. As one college manager put it: 'Challenging behaviour in college is very different to what Social Services mean by challenging behaviour!' The lack of a shared terminology can prove to be an obstacle to effective collaboration. Expectations may also vary. In one case, a health trust manager was alarmed to find that a resident's behaviour had actually deteriorated significantly since going to college, yet the college's view was that everything was fine.

There may also be a problem with history and 'baggage'. One college wanted to develop provision for adults with the most severe learning difficulties and disabilities. There was initially some animosity from Social Services staff, who remembered vividly a failed experience from several years previously. This had to be brought up and the air cleared before new developments could be planned.

Re-organisations, cuts in services and inspections can also have an impact generally on one or more partner organisations. Sometimes it can be frustrating to feel that it seems as if your organisation is the only one making an effort. As one person said: 'It all seems to come from the college.'

▶ Summary

Most examples of education for under-represented groups of adults with learning difficulties were built on partnerships.

There are advantages in joint funding, working and training.

Liaison across agencies takes time and this should be reflected in job descriptions, adjusting the timetabling/teaching loads as appropriate.

Difficulties included clash of planning cycles, different understandings of language, and differing priorities and expectations.

Making it happen – a checklist of ideas

Joint planning

▶ Is continuing education included in your local authority's Community Care plan?

▶ If not, can you talk to a contact who works for the local authority and your own colleagues about how to get involved?

▶ Are the Community Care plan targets taken account of in your organisation's strategic plan?

▶ Are senior staff from you organisation involved in Community Care planning sub-groups?

Developing links

▶ Who are your current partners in joint work?

▶ Is there anyone else you could be working with?

▶ What are the pros and cons of joint working?

Working together effectively

 Below is a list of some key factors involved in working together effectively. How much are they a part of your joint working arrangements?

- Good communication
- Adequate time for liaison and networking built into staff roles
- A key person in an organisation to liaise with about day-to-day matters
- Support from senior management
- Opportunities for joint staff development
- Planning time together
- A shared philosophy and approach to working with students with learning difficulties from marginalised groups
- Mutual trust
- Respect for each other's skills
- Providing opportunities, if appropriate, to share skills and expertise.

REFERENCES/RESOURCES

Inclusive Learning, Report of the Committee on Students with Learning Difficulties and/or Disabilities (1996, FEFC)

The Learning Age: a renaissance for a new Britain (1998, DfEE).

Jeannie Sutcliffe, *Module 4 of Enabling Learning, A Student-Centred Approach to Teaching Adults with Learning Difficulties* (1996, NIACE).

8

Staff development and training

'Staff training should be like some of our training, about people's rights. Looking at different rights like civil and human rights. Training for college staff should be about helping people with learning difficulties and their behaviours. If they are having trouble understanding a document, try and make it more accessible for everyone in the class.'
(Justine March from CHANGE)

'Training should be about deaf awareness, civil rights and making the actual course more accessible.'
(Paul Adeline from CHANGE)

Paul and Justine, workers with learning difficulties at CHANGE, both have very clear ideas about what staff need to learn. It has been recognised by the *Inclusive Learning* report and also by the Special Educational Needs Training Consortium (SENTC) that staff training and development in relation to education for adults with learning difficulties and/or disabilities is uncharted territory. There is no coherent or national programme of staff training and development in this area. To this end, the Further Education Funding Council in

England is investing heavily in a programme of staff development and materials generation called the Quality Initiative. The long-term plan is to have training opportunities available at all levels in relation to inclusive learning, which will be tied into an accreditation framework.

It will obviously take time for these developments to materialise. It is worth pointing out that, with staff training being limited anyway, opportunities which relate to marginalised groups of adults with learning difficulties are virtually non-existent. In the meantime, what forms of staff training and development are being used?

In-house

Many colleges and LEAs run their own training in-house. This can vary from weekly sessions targeted at small groups of staff through to closing the college for a day for all staff to learn more about working with students with learning difficulties. Sometimes colleagues from different agencies are invited in to run training sessions.

To give an example of one college's approach, Hertford Regional College has run staff training in relation to working with students with profound and multiple learning difficulties which has included the following:

- training on visual impairment from a mobility officer
- training on multi-sensory disabilities from a SENSE specialist
- inputs on curriculum from the local school
- joint training with Social Services staff
- speech therapy input in return for training given by the college
- challenging behaviour workshop
- particular short courses designed by the college, such as 'working with individuals'.

Support staff are offered the City and Guilds courses 7321/01 or

7321/02, described later in this chapter. College staff have also used a course run by St Andrew's University, which has a multi-disciplinary approach and an emphasis on people with profound and multiple learning difficulties.

User-led training at Lambeth Community Education

Lambeth Community Education is unusual in that it offers a training course which is co-tutored by people with learning difficulties. It is aimed at tutors, support staff and others working with people who have learning difficulties, such as social workers. The course runs over 15 weeks and has inputs from three people with learning difficulties. Raymond Johnson, for example, trains people from his perspective of being a black person with learning difficulties. Raymond asks staff questions to get them to consider issues such as positive images, tackling racism, and differences between various ethnic groups in relation to topics such as diet, dress, religion, hair and skin care. Vic Forrest, the tutor responsible for the work, is currently seeking accreditation for the course.

Training for Change

NIACE recognised that people with learning difficulties are increasingly being asked to deliver training, but that there were no materials to support people to develop the skills. Working in partnership with CHANGE, NIACE has produced a pack called *Training for Change*. Some learners who want to use the pack may be non-readers, while others may have an additional sensory impairment. Therefore, the pack is fully illustrated and is also accompanied by a video and audio-tapes, to make it as accessible as possible for all learners. This development work was supported by the Department of Health and by the National Lottery Charities Board. We hope that colleges and adult education centres will want to run the course.

Securing National Open College Network accreditation for the course was a logical progression. With help from the Open College Network of the South West, the 15 modules in the pack have been translated to offer five units at Entry Level or Level One for National Open College Network accreditation. A NOCN national award is available called Training for Change.

Initial tutor training

Postgraduate Certificate of Education (PGCE) A few places offer full-time one-year courses which specialise in further education and working with people with learning difficulties, such as the Bolton Institute of Higher Education and the University of Greenwich.

The Further and Adult Education Teacher's Certificate (City and Guilds 7306/7307) This is a general course for tutors working in adult and continuing education, which is not specifically for tutors working with students with learning difficulties. However, there is an opportunity on the course to specialise in a relevant subject area. For example, Solihull College and North Birmingham College both have staff from their learning support teams on this course. It is studied in-service.

Continuing Professional Development (Special Needs) City and Guilds 7401 This course is for people who already have a teaching qualification. Richmond Adult Education Service has just started using this course and the City of Liverpool Community College also uses it. However, it is not specifically for staff who work with students with learning difficulties.

Support worker training

Training of support staff is a key issue, as highlighted in Chapter 6 on support:

- All support staff at the City of Liverpool Community College have an induction training. The induction manual provided for this training was produced by support workers. This *Effective Support in Learning, Support Workers' Handbook*

Code of practice for support workers

In Southwark, health authority support workers accompanied some people with learning difficulties to their adult education classes. The students had recently resettled back into the local community after leaving long-stay hospital. Adult education staff developed a code of practice for the support workers. The code of practice sought to consolidate a training session led by adult education staff for the health authority induction programme that all new support workers attended.

The code of practice breaks down the worker's role by looking at the support they need to offer to the student before, during and after the class.

Before the class:
- preparing for the journey, leaving enough time, perhaps learning the route beforehand
- helping the student organise things needed for the class, money for break, equipment, appropriate clothes.

During the class:
- encouraging the student to participate
- acting as a role model
- offering choice to the student at every opportunity
- always checking with the student if they need help.

After the class:
- encouraging the transfer of learning after the class e.g. cooking a dish at home that was learned in the cookery class.
- giving the student the opportunity to reflect on the things they liked and/or didn't like about the class.
- monitoring with the student and tutor the level of support needed as the student progresses in class.

includes information on good practice for support, barriers to Inclusive Learning, ways to overcome these barriers, and details of a mentoring scheme where new staff are supported by permanent Educational Support Workers.

- At Blackburn College, several support workers are learning British Sign Language and a course for deaf/blind communication is being set up.

City and Guilds courses for support staff These courses are fairly widely used. There are two Learning Support courses. The Certificate in Learning Support (7321/01) is an introductory course. This course is for learning support staff in general, not just for staff working with students with learning difficulties. The course can be run for staff working in schools and FE. The course usually runs over six months as weekly sessions of three hours, but could also be run over a year.

Course participants are assessed in the workplace and on a course portfolio. Thanet College runs the 7321/01 course for support staff from secondary schools and for staff in FE. It is part of the contract that college learning support staff working with students with learning difficulties should do the course. Jo Campbell of Thanet College feels that the course:

- gives an opportunity to get back into study
- broadens knowledge – the students on the course have a better concept of services available in the community
- increases confidence.

Several of the colleges visited run the 7321/01 course for staff working with students with learning difficulties. They have commented that:

- the course can be useful – especially if it is mainly run for staff working with adults with learning difficulties
- it can be quite difficult to make work relate to the course
- it can help staff to focus on the purpose of their role
- it is easily adaptable and very flexible.

However, another college feels that the course is too basic and prefers to use sections of the NIACE staff development pack *Enabling Learning*, which is specific to learning difficulties.

There is also a more advanced learning support course: the City and Guilds Advanced Certificate in Learning Support (7321/02), which is equivalent to an NVQ Level Three.

Other approaches to staff development

Here are some of the other ways in which people have extended their skills and knowledge:

NIACE Staff Packs

NIACE has produced two staff development packs:

- *Enabling Learning: A student-centred approach to teaching adults with learning difficulties*
- *Towards Inclusion: Developing integrated education for adults with learning difficulties*

Aimed at staff working with people with learning difficulties in continuing education, social services day centres, health trusts and voluntary organisations, the packs are presented in module form and can be studied throughout or dipped into. The packs are linked to Open College Network accreditation.

Distance learning

The University of Sheffield offers a Masters in Inclusive Education. The Open University's most recent course in relation to learning difficulties is called 'Equal People'. It is designed for people with and without learning difficulties to study side by side. It can be used for staff training of education and support staff. The pack is accredited by the National Open College Network and linked with vocational qualifications.

Attending conferences

Organisations such as NIACE, Further Education Development Agency (FEDA) and Skill (the National Bureau for Students with Disabilities) all regularly organise national conferences.

Attending short courses

For example, Orchard Hill College of Further Education in Carshalton, Surrey has started to offer workshops on working with students who have profound and multiple learning difficulties.

Other options

Job shadowing, secondments and mentoring systems have all been used to widen the experience and skills of staff.

▶ Summary

As the *Inclusive Learning* report points out, there is a huge gap in terms of staff development in relation to education and people with learning difficulties and/or disabilities.

The Further Education Funding Council's 'Quality Initiative' aims to lay the foundations of a coherent national system for staff development and training, linked to accreditation.

Meanwhile, staff are using a variety of ways to offer staff training. This includes in-house training and use of external courses.

However, there is little in the way of 'off the shelf' staff training that relates directly to working with marginalised groups of adults with learning difficulties.

Making it happen – a checklist of ideas

▶ What are the options for staff training in your organisation?

▶ Where are the strengths and the gaps?

▶ Are people with learning difficulties involved in running or designing any of the training?

▶ Can you use your contacts with other agencies to provided specialist training where appropriate?

▶ Does existing training address working with marginalised group of adults with learning difficulties?

▶ If not, would it be possible to set something up?

REFERENCES/RESOURCES

Professional Development to meet Special Educational Needs (1996, Special Educational Needs Training Consortium)

Enabling Learning, Staff development pack (1996, NIACE)

Towards Inclusion, Staff development pack (1996, NIACE)

Orchard Hill College of Further Education
6, Elm Avenue, Orchard Hill, Fountain Drive, Carshalton, Surrey SM5 4NR

Training for Change, A pack to support adults with learning difficulties to develop the skills to be trainers (1998, NIACE/CHANGE)

School of Health and Social Welfare
The Open University, Walton Hall, Milton Keynes MK7 6AA

User Involvement: Community Service Users as Consultants and Trainers. Published by the NHS Executive Community Care Branch 1996. Available from: Two Ten, Building 150, Thorp Arch Trading Estate, Wetherby, West Yorkshire LS23 7EH

9

Funding, progression and accreditation

'I was on a business studies NVQ I scheme. The work covered much of what I had experienced before – stock control, Health and Safety, photocopying, post room work. At times I found it difficult but we had to help each other. I needed two extensions, I had to write up a massive thing. I did do it successfully. I wouldn't recommend the course...it was badly run. It seemed as if the paper work was more important than the things being taught.'

(Student with learning difficulties and mental health difficulties)

Securing funding to develop provision is a concern for managers and staff. This chapter looks at the different ways in which the provision we visited was funded and how issues of progression and accreditation were dealt with.

Funding

Funding came from a variety of sources, which included:
*   The Further Education Funding Councils in England and Wales

- Local Education Authorities
- Social Services departments
- Health Authorities/Trusts
- Voluntary organisations.

Much funding was in partnership or involved sharing of resources. Although providers did not explicitly mention these funding sources to us, there may be scope in exploring European Community funding aimed at excluded groups, links with Training and Enterprise Councils and regeneration budgets.

For the purposes of Further Education Funding Council funding, progression must be demonstrated for courses listed under Schedule 2d (which are preparatory courses for vocational and academic courses) and 2j, which refers explicitly to courses in 'independent living and communication skills for students with learning difficulties'. Funding to cover support needed by individual students, known as additional support units, is central to much of the provision for students with learning difficulties funded by the FEFC.

Finding funding for support costs appeared to be more difficult for LEAs, especially in relation to non-vocational learning. LEAs were more likely to draw on volunteers to provide additional support than colleges were.

Adult education services in LEAs have faced massive budget cuts in recent years. During this project, major cuts in LEA adult education services closed a number of classes in one area at about the time we visited, including outreach provision for marginalised groups of adults with learning difficulties. In other areas, provision had been set up on a pilot basis and was potentially vulnerable to cuts, as it was perceived that senior managers saw the provision as being relatively unimportant.

However, one or two places had deliberately chosen to set up provision for marginalised groups with LEA funding so that there would be 'more flexibility...we didn't want to get into the cycle early on about progression and moving on.'

How can new opportunities be funded?

As there is so little work in existence with marginalised groups of adults with learning difficulties, it is worth pausing for a moment to think about possibilities for obtaining funding.

- Can other agencies or community organisations be approached for partnership work, funding or resources in kind? Many of the examples in this book are based on shared resourcing, shared tutoring or shared premises.
- Are any start-up funds available? It is a recommendation from *Inclusive Learning* that start up funds should be provided to reach under-represented groups. Other small grants may be available from time to time. For example, NIACE recently awarded small grants to 24 LEAs on the theme of extending learning communities, on behalf of the DfEE. In 1998, NIACE was asked to administer an adult and community learning fund by the DfEE, following the publication of the green paper *The Learning Age*. The fund is designed to support community-based learning, to include under-represented groups.
- Can existing resources be re-prioritised? Solihull College targeted people with challenging behaviour and people with mental health difficulties after an internal review of provision following the *Inclusive Learning* report.
- Has European Community funding been explored? For example, Mencap has recently been granted finance from Europe to run a project developing employment opportunities for women with learning difficulties.
- Can a bid for joint finance be made? One college supports people with the most severe disabilities on non-vocational courses with £100,000 of backing from Health and Social Services.

Progression

'I have been going to college on and off for ten years now...now I am doing a CLAIT (Computer Literacy & Information Technology) course in computers and it's been really good. I'm finishing it off next year and it's really good. I've been thinking about doing a GNVQ, everybody's talking about that...hopefully I will get some more information about that.'

(Maria, student with learning difficulties and mental health difficulties)

Progression can be defined in a number of ways, to include gaining new skills, developing confidence or moving on to a new course or to employment. One of the recommendations of the *Inclusive Learning* report was that progression should be re-interpreted by the FEFC to enable lateral progression and maintenance of skills, rather than relying solely on a vertical, ladder-like vision of progression. This recommendation is still under consideration by the FEFC at the time of writing.

Also under consideration by FEFC is a recommendation to expand opportunities for people with profound and multiple learning difficulties. In a landmark legal case in 1997, a judge upheld the decision of the FEFC to refuse funding to Robert Parkinson, a 19 year-old with profound and multiple learning difficulties. It was deemed that he would not demonstrate adequate progression, which brings back uncomfortable echoes of the term 'ineducable', which was in use until 1971. The existing funding arrangements do not disbar people with profound and multiple learning difficulties from participating in continuing education opportunities. However, many courses are not currently accessible either in terms of content or physical access which, coupled with the need to demonstrate progress, makes it hard for such learners to participate. The lack of opportunity effectively disenfranchises many potential learners who have profound and multiple learning difficulties.

Progression to other Schedule 2 courses is a requirement of FEFC funding for certain courses, under the FHE Act (1992). Progression must be demonstrated and documented under Schedule 2d and 2j, which relate to preparatory courses and to courses in independent living and communication skills for students with learning difficulties. Many providers feel that their provision is more secure if it is accredited, and there has been a surge of accreditation of learning. However, there is then a tension that the accreditation process can dominate the learning, rather than the student defining his/her own learning goals. These complexities are compounded by the fact that progression can sometimes be only in very small steps for a learner with profound and multiple learning difficulties, or can be intermittent for the person with learning difficulties who also has mental health problems.

There seems to be a general gap in terms of people with learning difficulties moving on from education to take up opportunities with supported employment organisations. Recent research found that only 8.3 per cent of all people with learning difficulties who joined supported employment schemes had come from colleges of further education (1997, Beyer, Goodere and Kilsby). It would be logical to assume that under-represented groups would miss out even more, as many of them do not have access to college in the first place.

Accreditation

Until recently, much work with adults with learning difficulties was not accredited. The rigour which accreditation has brought is welcomed, but there are lingering fears that it may still serve to exclude some learners, if only because there is some outstanding confusion about funding and accreditation issues as we explain later in this chapter.

'I am looking for any job or training jobs, maybe in September…
I have learnt a lot on motor vehicles but sometimes it is hard.'
(Deaf man with learning difficulties who has completed most of
an NVQ Level I in Motor Vehicle Maintenance)

'We like getting certificates!'
(Members of a self advocacy group)

The following ways of obtaining accreditation were reported to
us:

- via local Open College Network providers
- using Wordpower and Numberpower (Basic skills courses
  accredited by City & Guilds)
- using ASDAN programmes (modular programmes, where
  students can work with different levels of support as
  required)
- via the Northern Examinations and Assessment Board
  (NEAB)
- via the Northern Council for Further Education (NCFE)
- accessing National Vocational Qualifications (NVQs)
- using the National Skills Profile via the Royal Society of
  Arts
- via the National Proficiency Test Council (NPTC)
- using the Accreditation for Life and Living (ALL) via the
  Royal Society of Arts (RSA), which has been used for some
  students with profound and multiple learning difficulties.

One college manager told us: 'We won't accredit for the sake of
it. The inspectors talked about not giving brownie points for
people cleaning their teeth…'

In the book *Still A Chance to Learn?*, we reported the fears of
practitioners that the emphasis on progression and accredita-

tion would serve to exclude vulnerable learners, such as those with profound and multiple learning difficulties or older learners. The research found that some provision had been closed, as funding was either lost or jeopardised. During the work for *All Things Being Equal?*, we found that there was still a lot of confusion on the ground about what was acceptable to the Further Education Funding Council and what was not. For example, an FEFC inspector told us that accreditation was not a current requirement, as long as progression could be demonstrated. Yet several people had been told at a local level that accreditation was essential. Equally, a number of managers and practitioners were convinced that the FEFC would not fund learners over the age of 60, which was not, in fact, the case. Rumours and misinformation at a local level seemed to be a problem. Strategies for avoiding confusion include having a network of reliable contacts, sharing updates and double-checking information.

The emerging framework for entry level qualifications will be a factor in the future debate on qualifications and accreditation for students with learning difficulties, to include those from marginalised groups.

▶ Summary

Funding was provided from a number of sources. Sharing funding and/or resources was common.

Some funding was fragile, leading to some classes closed down during the course of the project *All Things Being Equal?*

A number of different sorts of accreditation were in use.

Many staff feel they have to offer accreditation in order to secure their provision. However, this can lead to skewing the learning to suit the paper work in cases where there is no scope for flexibility in the accreditation process.

Making it happen – a checklist of ideas

▶ How could resources be embedded or expanded to cater for marginalised groups of adults with learning difficulties in your area?

▶ Could the existing resources be used differently to enable under-represented groups to participate?

▶ How do you show progression?

▶ Do your methods of recording progression include photos, video, audio-tape, and portfolios?

▶ Which approaches to accreditation do you favour and why? Are there other approaches you could develop / pursue?

RESOURCES

Stephen Beyer, Lara Goodere and Mark Kilsby, *The costs and benefits of supported employment agencies* (1997, The Stationery Office)

10

A framework for change

The key message from *All Things Being Equal?* is that vulnerable groups of adults with learning difficulties are still missing out on education. This chapter reflects on main issues and some unresolved questions, before offering a self-assessment checklist which can be used as a basis to plan developments.

There are creative examples of practice, which have been documented in this book, but they are as yet few and far between. What can be done to broaden access for marginalised groups? It is to be hoped that the current tidal wave of policy initiatives, from widening participation to combating social exclusion and lifelong learning, can provide a backdrop for substantive developments. The evidence from research into the under-representation of certain groups (e.g. from *Mapping Provision* and from *Inclusive Learning*) may also be used as a tool in the case for developing provision.

Isolation was experienced by many of the practitioners and managers working with marginalised groups. Networking and sharing ideas can only help, as the project's three network meetings demonstrated. An e-mail discussion group on education for adults with learning difficulties has recently been proposed by NIACE: perhaps this may be one small step in the right direction.

Many examples of practice were dependent on the enthusiasm and dedication of one or two key individuals. Embedding equal opportunities for people with learning difficulties in education is essential, and linking with other equal opportunities initiatives certainly helped some colleagues to establish new provision, such as the Asian Studies course at South Nottingham College. Here the College's Equal Opportunities development team gave a great deal of support to the development of the course and contributed towards the cost of an external tutor from their budget.

It could be argued that some of the discrete provision which we have described militates against the ethos of full integration in the community. It is our belief that some of the most disenfranchised groups of adults with learning difficulties can gain strength and develop self-identity by, for example, meeting as black students together or as women together. We would see separate provision as a gateway to further, integrated learning opportunities rather than as an end in itself. Also for certain groups, such as the Asian women's group, meeting as a same-gender and shared language group proved to be the most appropriate learning environment. We need to reflect on the Tomlinson report definition of inclusive learning being a match between the learner, the learning environment and the task.

It is clear that there is a dearth of readily-available resources for work with older learners with learning difficulties or those from black and other ethnic minority groups. We heard about inappropriate junior school materials about wheatfields in Canada being used with one group of Asian women: neither age-appropriate nor culturally relevant.

It seems that there is, as yet, no clear consensus nationally about the most appropriate methods or environments to work with learners who have profound and multiple learning difficulties. Our project advisory group of adults with learning difficulties from CHANGE was alarmed to hear that people with profound and multiple learning difficulties were, in some cases, returning to hospitals where they had formerly lived in order to continue their learning. They said:

'If they were living away from the hospital they shouldn't have to go back again, once they have gone out of there they shouldn't have to go back. They should go to college like everyone else.'

'They should have the opportunity to go to college. If they go back into the hospital, it's not going to feel any different.'

There are also unanswered questions in relation to the range of subjects which people can learn. Previous research (*Still A Chance to Learn?*, 1996) showed that the curriculum on offer had narrowed as places sought to obtain FEFC funding for strictly-defined list of Schedule 2 courses. Two years later, some areas of the curriculum still appear to be largely neglected, except for rare examples:

- **What about new technology and IT?** Thanet College was rare in having an IT and Internet course available for older learners with learning difficulties. The learners had made contact with Romania, amongst other places.
- **Where does self-advocacy fit into the framework?** It is especially important for marginalised groups. One self-advocacy course for black students with learning difficulties had been thriving. However, it changed to become a Popular Culture course for accreditation purposes, and in doing so apparently 'lost its focus'.
- **NIACE has always advocated access to the widest possible curriculum** for all adults with learning difficulties. People with learning difficulties are learning culturally diverse subjects such as Hebrew, Indian cookery and Welsh, but these are isolated examples.

Working across agencies was a recurrent theme of the provision visited, whether it was aimed at black or Asian students or at people with profound and multiple learning difficulties. Outreach work and time for liaison were essential, which is a factor to consider in planning developments.

The whole area of staff development and training is long overdue for change. We welcome the fact that the FEFC's 'Quality Initiative' will extend to LEAs and other organisations. A similar initiative is needed in Wales. If not, we are in danger of creating a two-tier system of staff development which will benefit only some staff and learners.

Lifelong learning is the new mantra in continuing education. How can we work together to make lifelong learning a reality for students with learning difficulties, irrespective of race, gender, age or disability?

A framework for change: developing provision for marginalised groups of adults with learning difficulties

This **self-assessment checklist** is designed to help people to reflect on progress towards including marginalised groups and individuals with learning difficulties in continuing education. It could be used to set an action plan, with dates and targets added. Tick one box for each item, after considering whether each aspect of developing provision is:

1   Non-existent
2   Under-developed
3   Developed
4   Well-developed

1 2 3 4

Awareness of national reports/policy directions

☐☐☐☐ Are you and other staff in your organisation aware of key messages/ summaries from national reports such as *Inclusive Learning* and *Widening Participation*?

☐☐☐☐ Has your organisation responded to the green paper *The Learning Age* with reference to learners with learning difficulties and/or disabilities?

Policy in your organisation

☐☐☐☐ Is including marginalised groups and widening participation a stated policy objective for your organisation?

1 2 3 4

☐☐☐☐ Is it included in your organisation's strategic plan and the disability statement?

Needs analysis

☐☐☐☐ Has a mapping exercise taken place to establish what gaps there are in provision?

☐☐☐☐ Does this include people who may face multiple discrimination, such as Asian women with learning difficulties?

Does your organisation offer provision for adults with learning difficulties who:

☐☐☐☐ are older?

☐☐☐☐ have profound/multiple learning difficulties?

☐☐☐☐ are from black or other minority ethnic groups?

☐☐☐☐ are women?

☐☐☐☐ present what has been described as challenging behaviour?

☐☐☐☐ have additional sensory disabilities?

☐☐☐☐ have both learning difficulties and mental health difficulties?

☐☐☐☐ have a history of institutionalisation?

Ways into education

☐☐☐☐ What access routes into education are available in your area for under-represented groups of adults with learning difficulties?

Curriculum

☐☐☐☐ How wide is your curriculum offer for students with learning difficulties from marginalised groups?

☐☐☐☐ Does the curriculum reflect minority ethnic group representation and cultural differences as appropriate for your local area?

1 2 3 4

Self-advocacy
☐☐☐☐ What self-advocacy provision is available in continuing education for students with learning difficulties from marginalised groups in your area?

Consultation
☐☐☐☐ What consultation mechanisms exist with community groups and user groups of people with learning difficulties and/or disabilities?

User involvement
☐☐☐☐ How are users involved in designing and evaluating provision?

Accessible information
Do you provide information which is :
☐☐☐☐ in large print?
☐☐☐☐ illustrated?
☐☐☐☐ on video?
☐☐☐☐ on audio-tape?
☐☐☐☐ on CD Rom?
☐☐☐☐ translated into relevant community languages?

Accessible buildings
☐☐☐☐ How accessible are your buildings?
☐☐☐☐ What improvements are planned?
☐☐☐☐ What can be done at low cost or no cost?

Resources
☐☐☐☐ Has a resource bank of appropriate materials been developed?
(This could include, for example, positive images of black students and older students.)

Transport
☐☐☐☐ Have you assessed and logged current difficulties with transport?

1 2 3 4

☐☐☐☐ Do you have a coherent transport policy across agencies?
☐☐☐☐ Do you have a plan for action to improve transport?

Senior management support

☐☐☐☐ Do you have the active support of senior managers?
☐☐☐☐ Is there scope for awareness raising?

Student support structures

☐☐☐☐ Do you have adequate student support structures in place?
☐☐☐☐ Is first-language support available as required for students with learning difficulties from minority ethnic groups?
☐☐☐☐ Is English for Speakers of Other Languages (ESOL) provision available as required for students with learning difficulties from ethnic minorities?

Inter-agency collaboration

☐☐☐☐ Is your organisation involved in joint planning?
☐☐☐☐ Is continuing education included in the Community Care plan?

Staffing

☐☐☐☐ Is staffing relevant to the needs of the learners?
☐☐☐☐ Are staff from black or other minority ethnic groups employed to teach adults with learning difficulties from black or other ethnic minority groups?
☐☐☐☐ Are deaf staff employed to teach deaf adults with learning difficulties?

Staff development framework

☐☐☐☐ What staff development opportunities are there in relation to working with marginalised groups?
☐☐☐☐ Is training offered to support staff both in-house and from other agencies?
☐☐☐☐ Are relevant books and resources available for staff?

1 2 3 4

Staff support structures

☐☐☐☐ How are staff given ongoing support, particularly if they work in isolated settings?

Flexible working

☐☐☐☐ Are time and resources dedicated to outreach work?

☐☐☐☐ Can key staff attend inter-agency planning meetings as part of their job descriptions?

Funding

☐☐☐☐ How secure is funding for developments in this area of work?

☐☐☐☐ How can it be embedded/consolidated?

☐☐☐☐ Are there joint funding arrangements with other agencies?

☐☐☐☐ Have European funding options been explored?

Fees

☐☐☐☐ Do you have a policy of fee remission for students on low incomes?

☐☐☐☐ Is there help with the cost of course materials for students on low incomes?

Useful addresses

CHANGE
First Floor
69-85 Old Street
LONDON EC1V 9HY
Tel: 0171 490 2668

Further Education Development Agency
Dumbarton House
68 Oxford Street
LONDON W1N 0DA
Tel: 0171 436 0020

Further Education Funding Council
Cheylesmore House
Quinton Road
COVENTRY CV1 2WT
Tel: 01203 863000

Further Education Funding Council for Wales
Linden Court, The Orchards
Ty Glas Avenue
Llanishen
CARDIFF CF4 5GL
Tel: 01222 761861

Joseph Rowntree Foundation
The Homestead
40 Waterend
YORK YO30 6WP
Tel: 01904 629241

Mencap National Centre
123 Golden Lane
LONDON EC1Y 0RT
Tel: 0171 454 0454

NIACE: The National Organisation for Adult Learning
21 De Montfort Street
LEICESTER LE1 7GE
Tel: 0116 204 4200

Open University
Walton Hall
MILTON KEYNES MK7 6AA
Tel: 01908 274066

Pavilion Publishing (Brighton) Ltd
8 St George's Place
BRIGHTON
East Sussex BN1 4GB
Tel: 01273 623222

People First
Instrument House
207-15 Kings Cross Road
LONDON WC1X 9DB
Tel: 0171 713 6400

RNIB
224 Great Portland Street
LONDON W1N 6AA
Tel: 0171 388 1266

Skill
National Bureau for Students with Disabilities
336 Brixton Road
LONDON SW9 7AA
Tel: 0171 274 0565

Values Into Action (VIA)
Oxford House
Derbyshire Street
LONDON E2 6HG
Tel: 0171 729 5436